BEST *of the* BEST *from*
Dogwood Delights
COOKBOOK

**The Most Popular Recipes
from the Four Classic
Georgia Pioneers Cookbooks**

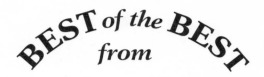

BEST of the BEST from
Dogwood Delights
COOKBOOK

**The Most Popular Recipes
from the Four Classic
Georgia Pioneers Cookbooks**

COMPILED BY
AT&T Pioneers of Georgia

PUBLISHED BY
QUAIL RIDGE PRESS
Preserving America's Food Heritage

Library of Congress Cataloging-in-Publication Data

Best of the best from dogwood delights cookbook : the most popular recipes from the four classic
    Georgia pioneer cookbooks / compiled by AT&T Pioneers of Georgia.
      p. cm.
    Includes index.
    ISBN-13: 978-1-934193-39-6
    ISBN-10: 1-934193-39-9
    1. Cookery, American. I. AT & T TelecomPioneers of Georgia.
    TX715.B4856145 2009
    641.5973--dc22   2009037236

ISBN-13: 978-1-934193-39-6 • ISBN-10: 1-934193-39-9

First printing, November 2009
Printed by Tara TPS in South Korea

Cover photo by Greg Campbell

On the cover: Apricot Ribs (page 165), Sausage Stuffed Vidalia Onions (page 120), Sweet Potato Soufflé (page 117), Cheese and Bacon Muffins (page 49), Vegetable Salad (page 95), Triple Chocolate S'More Pie (page 259), and Easy Peach Cobbler (page 262)

QUAIL RIDGE PRESS
P. O. Box 123 • Brandon, MS 39043 • 1-800-343-1583
email: info@quailridge.com • www.quailridge.com

Contents

Pioneering in Georgia

Pioneers are the world's largest corporate volunteer organization. Founded in 1911 as the Telephone Pioneers of America, we're now more than 620,000 members strong—men and women committed to serving our communities in the United States, Canada and beyond.

Pioneers are a network of volunteers who effect immediate, tangible change in local communities, in partnership with their sponsors. For nearly a century, the Pioneers volunteer network has logged hundreds of millions of hours meeting specific needs in local communities.

Whether it's a cash donation to support a homeless shelter, or a one-on-one tutoring project to battle illiteracy, Pioneers make it possible for sponsor companies to get involved with communities they are in—giving back to their customer base, while building their pool of potential employees.

The Georgia Chapter consists of over 22,000 dedicated men and women who come together as a team to "Improve the Quality of Life in our Communities." Made up of nineteen different units, our Regular Members, Pioneer Partners, and Life Members exemplify people caring about people throughout Georgia.

For more information on the Georgia Pioneers, please visit www.attpioneervolunteers.org/Georgia124/indexGA124.html.

Chapter 124

"Reaching Georgians through Community Service and Education"

at&t pioneers
a volunteer network

Preface

When BellSouth merged with AT&T on December 29, 2006, they combined two outstanding Telecommunications organizations that promised a new era of communications and entertainment for millions of people around the globe. This union not only merged our two businesses, it also merged our great volunteer organizations—The AT&T Pioneers.

You will find some fantastic recipes with this merging of four cookbooks from Legacy AT&T and Legacy BellSouth with the creation of the *Best of the Best from Dogwood Delights Cookbook.*

Since the first edition was published in 1984, our cookbooks have been profitable venues for the Georgia Pioneers. While the original *Dogwood Delights* (which had 1,690 recipes) was the most popular, the other books have also found their way into tens of thousands of households.

Dogwood Delights Volume II contained 1,053 recipes, and its proceeds went to 86 different charities throughout the state of Georgia. In 1992, *Lawfully Good Eating* was published by the Dixie Chapter #23 Telephone Pioneers of America. Then in 2004, the South Chapter #127 of AT&T Pioneers published *Great Southern Recipes from AT&T TelecomPioneers.*

Customers have praised the recipes found in all four cookbooks. In fact, people have enjoyed the meals prepared using these cookbooks so much that the requests for a book that combines the "Best of the Best" recipes has been a constant refrain from many of these cooks. Especially since all four original cookbooks are out of print, this book brings the best of them back by popular demand. Now Pioneers across the state of Georgia have submitted their selections of time-tested and proven recipes from all four books. These selections were compiled, sorted, and edited, and now grace the pages of this cookbook as a collection of the best recipes of the DOGWOOD DELIGHTS COOKBOOK SERIES.

This compilation is possible due to the countless hours of work by many active and retired Pioneers over the years. We dedicate this cookbook to the thousands of volunteers who make up the

Preface

AT&T Family and have shared their recipes. We hope that you enjoy them as much as our members have. Thank you for your support. Our proceeds will be used to support the various organizations in our Georgia communities.

It has been a joy working on this project with the "Best of the Best" Georgia Pioneers and the staff at Quail Ridge Press. We expect this book to be the next essential cookbook for every household.

Mandy A. Fridge

Mandy A. Fridge, 2009 President
GA Chapter #124 AT&T Pioneers

Cookbook Committee Members:
    Mandy Fridge
    Dorothy Fulcher
    Valerie Green
    Eddie Hindman
    Fran McNair
    Keith Pounds
    Cherry Strickland
    Phyllis Yancey

Quail Ridge Press was honored to be able to participate in the development and publication of the *Best of the Best from Dogwood Delights Cookbook.*

The down-home, family-favorites in the Georgia Pioneers cookbooks are exactly the kind of recipes we seek to preserve—recipes that have been developed and perfected over generations; recipes that are legendary within a family and are now being shared with other families.

Each Georgia Pioneers cookbook has been reprinted many times. The total sales of all four titles exceed well over 91,000 copies. The cookbooks continue to be popular with young cooks as well as long-time cooks.

The AT&T Pioneers of Georgia, the organization of employees, retirees, and families of the telecommunications industry in Georgia, are the force that have made the *Dogwood Delights* cookbooks the success they are. The Pioneers are all volunteers who have given their time and energy to a variety of projects and activities that enrich our community.

I speak for all of us at Quail Ridge Press in saying that we are proud to be a part of this new cookbook that offers the finest recipes from the DOGWOOD DELIGHTS COOKBOOK SERIES. This new cookbook will continue to provide the Pioneers with the revenue that finances their worthy projects and will enable Quail Ridge Press to continue our goal of Preserving America's Food Heritage.

Gwen McKee, President
Quail Ridge Press
Brandon, Mississippi

Dogwood Delights

After returning from the 1983 Annual Pioneer Assembly, the Dogwood Chapter #84 Telephone Pioneers of America started to work on their first cookbook *Dogwood Delights*, only to discover their large box full of recipes had been mistaken for trash and destroyed! In true resilient Pioneer fashion, the cookbook team started over from scratch and the first printing was completed in 1984. *Dogwood Delights* sold 49,000 copies, and was our most popular cookbook.

Dogwood Delights II

After an overwhelming response to *Dogwood Delights*, *Dogwood Delights Volume II* was published by the Dogwood Chapter #84 Telephone Pioneers of America in 1991. Over 20,000 copies of Volume II have been sold with the proceeds going to 86 different charities throughout the state of Georgia.

Great Southern Recipes

Great Southern Recipes from AT&T TelecomPioneers was published by the South Chapter #127 of AT&T TelecomPioneers in 2004. The recipes were submitted by members of the South Chapter, which covered the nine Southeastern states—from Florida to Kentucky and from North Carolina to Louisiana. The book contains 444 tried-and-true recipes. The proceeds from the book sales were used to fund numerous projects within our communities.

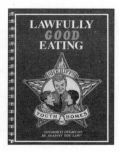

Lawfully Good Eating

Lawfully Good Eating was published by the Dixie Chapter #23 Telephone Pioneers of America in 1992. The proceeds from the 20,000+ books sold were donated to the Georgia Sheriffs Youth Homes, Inc.

Beverages and Appetizers

1876
Bell's Centennial Model

"My word! It talks!" exclaimed Emperor Dom Pedro of Brazil when this early phone was demonstrated by Alexander Graham Bell at the Centennial Exposition in Philadelphia on June 25, 1876. One of the judges called the invention "the most wonderful thing in America." Bell's success with the telephone came as a direct result of his attempts to improve the telegraph.

Just three months prior, while working with fellow inventor Thomas Watson, Bell shouted, "Mr. Watson, come here. I want you!" after spilling battery acid on a transmitter. Watson, working in the next room, heard Bell's voice through the wire. Watson had received the first telephone call, and quickly went to answer it.

Punch

3 gallons water, divided
3 (6-ounce) packages Jell-O
  (color of choice)
6 cups sugar
3 (46-ounce) cans unsweetened
  pineapple juice
3 (6-ounce) cans frozen orange
  juice
2 (6-ounce) cans frozen
  lemonade
3 (1-quart) bottles ginger ale,
  chilled
Garnishes: mint leaves, lemon
  slices, maraschino cherries

Heat 3 cups water to boiling. Remove from stove and add Jell-O and sugar; stir till dissolved. Add remaining ingredients except ginger ale and mix well. Just before serving, add chilled ginger ale. Float mint leaves, lemon slices, or maraschino cherries for garnish. Serves 150.

Sarah Bradley, General (Dogwood Delights)

Easy Punch

1 cup sugar
2 envelopes lemon-lime drink
  mix
1 (46-ounce) can pineapple
  juice
2 quarts cold water
1 cup bottled lemon juice
1 quart ginger ale
2 quarts slivered ice

Dissolve sugar and drink mix in pineapple juice in punch bowl. Add cold water and lemon juice; mix well. Add ginger ale and ice just before serving, stirring gently to mix. Yields 25 (6-ounce) servings.

Frances Hixon, Augusta Life Member Club
(Lawfully Good Eating)

Russian Tea Mix

½ cup instant tea mix with
   lemon
2 cups Tang
1 (3-ounce) package dry
   lemonade mix with sugar

½ teaspoon ground cloves
1 teaspoon ground cinnamon
Pinch of salt

Mix all ingredients together and store in airtight container. Mix 2 teaspoons per cup of boiling water. Add sugar, if needed.

Reba Bradley, General (Dogwood Delights)

Spiced Tea

3–4 lemons
12 cloves
1 quart water
3 cups sugar

2 quarts tea
1 (½ gallon) carton no-pulp
   orange juice

In large saucepan, squeeze lemon juice over cloves. Add lemon rinds and water; boil a few minutes. Let steep. Strain into large container. Add sugar, tea, and orange juice. Mix well, refrigerate. Heat as needed.

Diane Morris, General (Dogwood Delights)

The Best Eggnog

FOR SMALL SERVING:

¾ cup sugar
3 eggs
5–7 ounces whiskey
Pinch of salt

½ teaspoon vanilla
1½ cups milk
1 cup crushed ice
Nutmeg to taste

Blend all ingredients on high speed. Serve.

FOR VERY LARGE SERVING:

2½ dozen eggs, separated
6½ cups sugar, divided
3–4 cups whiskey
Dash of salt

2 tablespoons vanilla
1 gallon milk
Nutmeg to taste

In large blender, beat egg yolks; gradually add 6 cups sugar. Add whiskey, then salt, vanilla, milk, and nutmeg.

In separate container, beat egg whites. Add remaining ½ cup sugar gradually. Pour boiling water around outside of container. Leave for about 2 minutes. Remove from water. Add egg whites to eggnog mixture.

Sandy Saxton, General (Dogwood Delights II)

Has any means of communication revolutionized the daily lives of ordinary people more than the telephone? Simply described, it is a system which converts sound, specifically the human voice, to electrical impulses of various frequencies and then back to a tone that sounds like the original voice.

Cheese Ball

4 (8-ounce) packages cream
cheese, softened
1 (8-ounce) package grated
sharp Cheddar cheese, room
temperature
1 (6-ounce) jar smoked or
chipped beef, diced fine

2 tablespoons Worcestershire
¼ cup pickle relish
⅛ teaspoon Tabasco
¼ teaspoon onion salt
Dash of white pepper
Chopped parsley or grated
pecans for garnish

Cream cheeses; mix in remaining ingredients, except garnish, mixing well. Form into ball, and roll in parsley or pecans.

Cathye McDonals, General (Dogwood Delights)

Fruited Cheese Ball

2 (8-ounce) packages cream
cheese, softened
1 (20-ounce) can crushed
pineapple, drained
1 cup each: coconut and raisins

½ cup chopped dates
1 cup powdered sugar
Juice of ½ lemon
1 teaspoon vanilla
Chopped pecans

Combine all ingredients except pecans; mix well. Shape into ball. Refrigerate till firm. Roll in pecans at serving time. Yields 16 servings.

Linda Thompson, Albany Council (Lawfully Good Eating)

Pineapple Cheese Ball

2 (8-ounce) packages cream
  cheese, softened
1 (8-ounce) can crushed
  pineapple, drained
¼ cup finely chopped green
  bell pepper

2 tablespoons chopped onion
1 tablespoon seasoned salt
2 cups chopped pecans, divided

Combine all ingredients except 1 cup pecans. Mix well; refrigerate till firm, then shape into ball. Roll in remaining pecans. Serve with crackers.

Jean Hundley, Austell-Marietta (Dogwood Delights II)

Cheese Ring

1 pound finely grated Cheddar
  cheese
1 cup chopped pecans
1 cup mayonnaise

1 small onion, grated
Dash of cayenne pepper
Strawberry preserves

Mix together all except preserves. Shape into ring. Fill center of ring with strawberry preserves.

Betty Fox, Austell-Marietta (Dogwood Delights)

Cheese Straws

1 pound sharp Cheddar cheese,
  grated
1 stick margarine, softened
2 cups all-purpose flour, sifted

1 teaspoon salt
¼ teaspoon cayenne pepper, or
  to taste
½ cup chopped nuts (optional)

Mix cheese and margarine well. Gradually add flour, salt, and cayenne pepper to mixture. Thoroughly mix, adding nuts, if desired. Use cookie press, or pinch off about 2 inches of dough and press with fork tines.

Preheat oven to 350° and cook approximately 10 minutes or till lightly browned. This recipe can be made in food processor or mixer. Yields approximately 40 dozen.

Frances Hewin, Brookwood-Downtown (Dogwood Delights)

Cheese Log

2 (8-ounce) packages cream
  cheese, softened
2 teaspoons Worcestershire
1 teaspoon garlic salt, or ½
  teaspoon onion salt

Dash of Ac'cent
2 teaspoons lemon juice
2 packages chipped beef, diced

Mix all ingredients except chipped beef well. Wet hands in cold water; roll ingredients together into log. Spread chipped beef on wax paper; roll log in chipped beef. Place in refrigerator. Remove 30 minutes before serving. Serve with wheat toast.

Jean Hundley, Austell-Marietta (Dogwood Delights II)

Olive Cheese Spread

1½ cups grated sharp Cheddar
   cheese
½ cup minced green onions
1 cup chopped ripe olives

½ teaspoon chili powder
¼ teaspoon salt
½ cup mayonnaise

Mix all ingredients well. Spread on crackers or buttered thin white bread, toasted. Cut any shape you prefer. Spread and heat. Mixture can be kept in refrigerator for several days.

Sandy Duncan, Brookwood-Downtown (Dogwood Delights)

Ham Dip

½ cup mayonnaise
1 (7-ounce) can deviled ham
2 tablespoons chopped
   pimentos
1 (8-ounce) package cream
   cheese, softened

1 tablespoon grated onion
1 teaspoon parsley flakes
   (optional)
Worcestershire to taste
Salt and pepper to taste

Combine all ingredients; mix well. Spoon into serving dish. Serve with crackers. Yields 2 cups.

Nana Jarriel, Macon Council (Lawfully Good Eating)

Ma's Mexican Cheese Dip

1 pound ground beef
1 pound hot sausage
16 ounces shredded Cheddar
  cheese
16 ounces hot Mexican Velveeta
  cheese

1 (4-ounce) can chopped chile
  peppers, or 1–2 teaspoons
  cayenne pepper

Brown beef and sausage; drain. Add remaining ingredients. Cook on low heat till cheese has melted. Serve in slow cooker/crockpot with chips.

Carrie M. Lampkin, Conyers, GA (Great Southern Recipes)

Layered Taco Dip

1 (8-ounce) package cream
  cheese, softened
1 (14-ounce) can chili without
  beans
½ (4-ounce) can green chiles

8 ounces shredded Monterey
  Jack cheese
1 (4-ounce) can sliced black
  olives
Chopped green onions

In oven-safe dish, layer ingredients as listed. Heat in 400° oven till cheese bubbles, usually 15–20 minutes. Serve hot with tortilla chips.

Peggy Hovorka, Lithonia, GA (Great Southern Recipes)

Chili Dip

½ pound ground beef
1 small green bell pepper,
  chopped
1 small onion, chopped
3 tablespoons chili powder,
  divided

1 (8-ounce) can tomato sauce
1 (15-ounce) can refried beans
1 teaspoon salt
1 cup sour cream
1 cup grated Cheddar cheese

Fry ground beef, pepper, and onion till browned. Drain, then add ½ the chili powder, tomato sauce, refried beans, and salt. Mix well and pour into casserole dish. Add remaining chili powder to sour cream and spread over bean mixture. Top with grated cheese. Heat at 325° about 30 minutes or microwave on MEDIUM-HIGH 10–12 minutes.

Barbara Camp, Austell-Marietta (Dogwood Delights II)

Zesty Artichoke Dip

2 (14-ounce) cans artichoke
  hearts, drained, chopped
1 cup mayonnaise

1 cup grated Parmesan cheese
Dash of garlic salt and Tabasco

Mix together all ingredients in greased casserole dish. Bake at 350° for 25 minutes. Serves 6–8. Serve with crackers.

Ellie Trimble, Brookwood-Downtown (Dogwood Delights)

Knorr Festive Broccoli Dip

1 (10-ounce) package frozen
  chopped broccoli
2 cups sour cream
½ cup mayonnaise

1 (2.4-ounce) package Knorr leek
  soup mix
1 (8-ounce) can water chestnuts,
  finely chopped

Thaw broccoli; drain on paper towels. Stir together sour cream, mayonnaise, and soup mix. Stir in broccoli and water chestnuts. Cover and refrigerate 2 hours. Stir before serving. Dip may be stored in refrigerator up to 3 days. Makes 4 cups.

Bettie Bell, Austell-Marietta (Dogwood Delights II)

Asparagus Dip

1 (14½-ounce) can asparagus
  spears, drained
1 cup sour cream
¼ teaspoon hot sauce

½ teaspoon dried dill weed
½ teaspoon Beau Monde
  seasoning (or Season-All)

Combine all ingredients in blender or food processor. Blend till smooth; chill. Serve with crackers or raw veggies.

Sharron Lathem, General (Dogwood Delights II)

Spinach Dip

1 (10-ounce) package frozen
   chopped spinach, thawed
1 cup sour cream
1 cup mayonnaise

1 envelope vegetable soup mix
1 small onion, chopped
1 (8-ounce) can water chestnuts,
   finely chopped

Combine spinach, sour cream, mayonnaise, soup mix, onion, and water chestnuts in bowl; mix well. Spoon into serving dish. Chill overnight. Serve with thin wheat crackers. Yields 12 servings.

Alisa Chandler, Athens-Gainesville Council (Lawfully Good Eating); JoAnne Paulin, General (Dogwood Delights)

Spinach Balls

2 (10-ounce) packages frozen
   chopped spinach
3 cups herb-seasoned stuffing
   mix
1 large onion, finely chopped

6 eggs, well beaten
¾ cup butter, melted
½ cup grated Parmesan cheese
1 teaspoon garlic salt
½ teaspoon thyme

Cook spinach; drain and squeeze dry. Combine with remaining ingredients. Shape into ¾-inch balls. Bake on lightly greased cookie sheet at 325° for 15–20 minutes. (Can be frozen on cookie sheets before baking. Remove after frozen and store in plastic bags. Thaw slightly; bake at 325° for 20–25 minutes.)

Maudene Benton, Brookwood-Downtown (Dogwood Delights)

Guacamole Dip

2 avocados
1 tablespoon lemon juice
1 tablespoon salt
1 teaspoon chili powder

1 hot pepper, chopped
2 tablespoons grated onion
1 tomato, chopped
Mayonnaise

Place all ingredient except mayonnaise in blender; blend well. Spread on plate and cover with a layer of mayonnaise. Chill. Stir before serving. Serve with scoops or tortilla chips.

Pam Cown, Long Lines-AT&T Communication
(Dogwood Delights)

Dill Dip for Raw Vegetables

1 cup mayonnaise
2 cups sour cream
2 tablespoons dried dill weed
1 tablespoon minced parsley

Salt to taste
Assorted vegetables sprinkled
  with lemon juice

Combine all ingredients except vegetables. Serve in bowl surrounded by vegetables.

Margie Linnartz, Brookwood-Downtown (Dogwood Delights)

Hot Crab Dip

1 (8-ounce) package cream
   cheese, softened
3 tablespoons mayonnaise
2 tablespoons white wine

1 teaspoon mustard
½ teaspoon sugar
½ teaspoon salt
1 pound crabmeat

Mix all ingredients in saucepan. Heat thoroughly. Pour into serving bowl and serve with crackers.

Vicki Sanders, W. E. -BLT/Cable (Dogwood Delights)

Crabmeat Bites

1 (7-ounce) can crabmeat
½ cup butter, softened
1 (5-ounce) jar sharp Cheddar
   cheese spread
¼ teaspoon garlic salt

¼ teaspoon seasoned salt
1½ teaspoons mayonnaise
1 (12-ounce) package English
   muffins, split

Combine all ingredients except muffins. Spread muffin halves with mixture. Cut each in quarters. Bake at 350° till bubbly. Serve hot. Makes 4 dozen.

Doris A. Thompson, Grayson, GA (Great Southern Recipes)

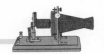

Crabmeat Spread

2 (8-ounce) packages cream
  cheese, softened
2 cups sour cream
2 teaspoons ranch salad
  dressing mix
1 teaspoon lemon-dill seasoning

1 package imitation crabmeat or
  lobster, coarsely chopped
1 bunch green onions, finely
  chopped
2 stalks celery, finely chopped

Process cream cheese and sour cream in food processor till smooth. Add salad dressing mix and seasoning; process till smooth. Add crabmeat, green onions, and celery; process just till mixed. Serve on crackers or small party rye bread slices. May also use as a dip. Yields 16 servings.

Linnea Grosse, Columbus Council (Lawfully Good Eating)

Bite-Sized Salmon Balls

1 (7¾-ounce) can salmon
1 egg, beaten
¼ cup mayonnaise
¼ cup shredded Cheddar
  cheese

1 cup crushed cheese crackers
¼ cup each: chopped dill
  pickles and olives

Mix all ingredients well. Shape into 1-inch balls. Place on cookie sheet and bake at 375° for 10–15 minutes till golden brown. Makes 5 dozen.

Helen Henderson, Brookwook-Downtown (Dogwood Delights)

Salmon Mold

1 (15-ounce) can pink or red
  salmon, drained, deboned
1 (8-ounce) package cream
  cheese, softened
1 tablespoon horseradish

1 small onion, grated
1 teaspoon lemon juice
Dash of liquid smoke
Tabasco (optional)

Mix all ingredients well. Mold in fish-shaped mold. To decorate (if desired) can use sliced stuffed olive for eye and sliced almonds for scales, sliver of red pimento for mouth. Place fresh parsley around to decorate and serve with soda crackers.

Marvella Garriss, Chamblee-North Fulton (Dogwood Delights)

Clam Rounds

Delicious!

1 (6-ounce) can clams, chopped
1 (8-ounce) package cream
  cheese, softened

Garlic salt to taste
Small bread rounds

Mix ingredients and spread on small bread rounds. Run in oven to heat. Serve hot.

Vera Ray, Chamblee-North Fulton (Dogwood Delights)

Shrimp Dip

1 (4-ounce) carton whipped
  cream cheese
½ cup salad dressing
1½ tablespoons lemon juice
½ cup chopped celery

¼ cup grated onion
2–3 dashes garlic salt
2 (4-ounce) cans shrimp,
  drained

Combine all ingredients except shrimp; chill 2 hours. Stir in shrimp and serve.

Mrs. James S. Holmes, General (Dogwood Delights)

Shrimp Mold

2 (7-ounce) cans shrimp
1 cup finely chopped celery
1 cup finely chopped green bell
  pepper
1 cup grated onion
¼ teaspoon salt
2 teaspoons lemon juice
1 teaspoon Worcestershire

½ teaspoon Tabasco
1 (10¾-ounce) can tomato soup
1 (8-ounce) package cream
  cheese
2 (3-ounce) packages unflavored
  gelatin
1 cup mayonnaise

Combine first 8 ingredients; mix well; set aside. Combine soup and cream cheese in double boiler. Heat till cheese melts. Soften gelatin in a little warm water; stir in with soup and cheese, then combine with all other ingredients, except mayonnaise. When mixture begins to thicken, blend in mayonnaise. Turn into lightly greased mold and chill.

Sandy Cook, Jonesboro-South Fulton (Dogwood Delights II)

Marinated Shrimp

3 pounds cooked, cleaned
  shrimp
1 cup French dressing
½ cup chopped green bell
  pepper
½ cup chopped onion

½ cup chopped parsley
1 clove garlic, crushed or
  pressed
2 tablespoons mustard
2 tablespoons lemon juice
Salt and pepper to taste

Combine all ingredients and marinate, refrigerated, at least 24 hours.

Kathryn Wallace, General (Dogwood Delights)

Shrimp Hots

1 (7-ounce) can small shrimp
1 cup shredded sharp Cheddar
  cheese
1 teaspoon horseradish

½–¾ cup mayonnaise
Salt and pepper to taste
Bread rounds

Chop shrimp; add cheese and horseradish. Blend with mayonnaise, salt and pepper. Spoon mixture onto small bread rounds. Bake at 400° for 5–10 minutes.

Doris Thompson, Grayson, GA (Great Southern Recipes)

Holiday Squares Florentine

4 eggs, beaten
1 (10¾-ounce) can cream of
   mushroom soup
2 (10-ounce) packages frozen
   chopped spinach, thawed,
   well drained, minced

½ cup chopped, toasted walnuts
¼ cup minced green onions
1 cup shredded Swiss cheese
¼ cup grated Parmesan cheese
1 (8-ounce) package refrigerated
   crescent rolls

Combine all ingredients except crescent rolls; mix well. Unroll crescent rolls, but do not separate. Press into bottom of 9x13-inch buttered baking pan. Press seams together. Spread spinach mixture over dough. Bake at 350° for 40 minutes or till knife inserted in center comes out clean. Cut into 1-inch pieces. Makes about 50 appetizers.

Ronda Little, Decatur-Tucker (Dogwood Delights II)

Onion Sausage Sticks

This is also good for a brunch or breakfast.

1½ cups finely chopped
   Spanish onion
1 cup buttermilk baking mix
½ teaspoon salt
4 eggs, beaten

½ pound bulk sausage, fried,
   drained
⅓ cup sausage drippings or oil
1 cup grated Cheddar cheese
2 tablespoons minced parsley

Combine all ingredients, mixing well. Spread in greased 9x13-inch baking pan. Bake at 350° for 20-25 minutes till golden. Let stand 5 minutes before cutting into sticks. Makes about 4 dozen.

Sue Storey, Decatur-Tucker (Dogwood Delights II)

Nacho Pie

1 (16-ounce) can refried beans
1 envelope taco seasoning mix, divided
½ cup mayonnaise
1 cup sour cream, divided
1 avocado
2 teaspoons lemon juice
1½ cups shredded medium Cheddar cheese, divided
2 tomatoes, chopped
Sliced black olives (optional)
1 cup shredded lettuce
½ cup chopped green onions

Mix beans with ⅓ of the taco seasoning mix. Spread in flat-bottomed dish. Combine mayonnaise with half the sour cream and half the remaining taco seasoning mix; mix well. Spread over bean layer. Mash avocado with lemon juice and remaining taco seasoning mix. Spread over sour cream layer. Sprinkle with ¾ cup cheese and olives. Sprinkle lettuce around edge of dish. Top with green onions. Serve with tortilla chips or large corn chips. Yields 16 servings.

Renita Anthony, Athens-Gainesville Council
(Lawfully Good Eating)

Ham Rolls

2 (8-ounce) packages cream cheese, softened
4 or 5 green onions with tops, chopped
12 rectangular slices sandwich ham
Round butter crackers

Combine cream cheese and green onions; mix well. Spread evenly on ham. Roll to enclose filling; secure with wooden picks, if necessary. Chill or freeze overnight.

Slice as desired. Serve on round butter crackers. Yields 12 servings.

Johnnie Driver, Athens-Gainesville Council
(Lawfully Good Eating)

Swiss Cheese-Ham Roll-Ups

1 (8-ounce) package tater tots
2 (2-ounce) slices Swiss
  cheese, cut in halves
4 (1-ounce) slices boiled ham
¼ cup sour cream

Microwave tater tots on paper plate on DEFROST till thawed. Place cheese on ham slices. Spread with sour cream. Top each slice with 3 tater tots. Roll to close filling. Secure with toothpick. Place on serving plate. Microwave, uncovered, 2 minutes or till heated through.

Maudene B. Benton, Central (Dogwood Delights II)

Asparagus Rolls

20 slices bread
1 egg, beaten
1 cup shredded sharp Cheddar
  cheese, softened
1 (8-ounce) package cream
  cheese, softened
1 (14-ounce) can asparagus
  spears, drained
1 cup margarine, melted

Trim crusts from bread. Flatten with rolling pin. Combine egg and softened cheeses; mix well. Spread evenly on bread. Place 1 asparagus spear on each slice of bread. Roll to enclose asparagus; secure with wooden picks. Dip in margarine; place on ungreased baking sheet. Freeze till firm.

Let stand at room temperature till partially thawed. Cut each roll into 3 pieces. Bake at 375° for 15 minutes, or till golden brown. Serve immediately. Makes 60.

Note: May substitute 3 ounces bleu cheese for Cheddar cheese.

Pat Hodges, Augusta Council (Lawfully Good Eating)

Meatball Treats

1 pound ground beef
1 envelope meatloaf mix

1 (9-ounce) bottle cocktail sauce
1 (6-ounce) jar grape jelly

Combine ground beef and meatloaf mix; mix well. Shape into small balls; place on baking sheet. Bake at 350° for 10 minutes or till cooked through; drain. Combine cocktail sauce and jelly in saucepan; mix well. Heat till smooth; add meatballs. Simmer 20–30 minutes, or till of desired consistency, stirring gently with wooden spoon. Yields 8 servings.

Virginia Archer, Athens-Gainesville Council
(Lawfully Good Eating)

Cocktail Meatballs

1 pound ground beef
⅓ cup chopped onion
½ cup bread crumbs
¼ cup milk

1 egg, beaten
½ teaspoon Worcestershire
Salt and pepper to taste

Combine all ingredients; roll into ½-inch balls. Brown in saucepan; set aside.

SAUCE:

2 or 3 (12-ounce) bottles
   cocktail or chili sauce

1 (10-ounce) jar grape jelly
Dash of barbecue sauce

Combine all ingredients in saucepan; simmer till melted. Place meatballs in Sauce. Serve warm. Can be frozen ahead of time.

Pearlie E. Riley, General (Dogwood Delights)

Spiced Meatballs

2 eggs, beaten
¾ cup finely crushed
   cornflakes
¾ cup grated Romano cheese
2 tablespoons snipped parsley
1 clove garlic, minced
¼ teaspoon salt

Dash of pepper, cinnamon,
   cloves, nutmeg
1 pound ground beef
¼ pound ground pork
2 tablespoons all-purpose flour
2 tablespoons cooking oil

Combine eggs, cornflakes, cheese, parsley, garlic, and seasonings; add to meats. Mix well. Shape mixture into 32 (1½-inch) meatballs. Coat with flour. In skillet brown meatballs, half at a time, in hot oil. Drain; reserve dripping after first batch. Makes 32 meatballs.

Susan Boone, W. E.-BTL/Cable (Dogwood Delights)

Sausage Balls

1 pound hot or regular pork
   sausage
1 pound sharp Cheddar cheese,
   grated

3 cups biscuit mix

Mix all ingredients well. Roll in balls about size of large marble. Bake on baking pan at 400° about 10 minutes or till brown. Keep warm in chafing dish. Makes about 190 appetizers.

Marlyn Long, Brookwood-Downtown (Dogwood Delights)

John's Bourbon Franks

½ cup ketchup
¾ cup bourbon
½ cup dark brown sugar
4 or 5 green onions, chopped

Red pepper to taste
4 packages cocktail wieners, or 4
   packages regular wieners, cut
   into 4 pieces

Combine and stir first 5 ingredients in a saucepan and heat to melt sugar. Put wieners in a large pot. Pour contents of saucepan over them. Simmer 1 hour, covered, stirring occasionally. Uncover and simmer 30 minutes, stirring more frequently to coat wieners with sauce.

John Sloan, Fayetteville, GA (Great Southern Recipes)

Buffalo Chicken Wings

24 chicken wings, washed,
   patted dry
Peanut oil for frying
1 stick margarine, melted
¼ cup vinegar

1 package Italian salad dressing
   mix
⅔ cup Durkee cayenne pepper
   sauce (no substitute)

Split wings at each joint. Discard tips. Heat oil in deep fryer to 375°. Fry 12–15 wings at a time in hot oil for 15–20 minutes or till golden brown. Drain on paper towels.

   Mix margarine, vinegar, dressing mix, and pepper sauce. Dip wings in sauce; drain and place on cookie sheet. Place in 150° oven; repeat with rest of wings. After last batch is coated with sauce, put all in oven for 15–20 minutes more. Serve with celery sticks and bleu cheese dressing.

Tony Kubiak, General (Dogwood Delights II)

Teriyaki Wings

⅓ cup lemon juice
¼ cup ketchup
¼ cup teriyaki sauce
2 tablespoons brown sugar
1 medium clove garlic, minced

¼ cup oil
¼ teaspoon pepper
3 pounds chicken wings, cut at
 joint and wing tips removed

Mix all ingredients except chicken to make marinade. Place chicken in 9x14-inch baking dish; pour marinade over chicken. Cover at least 6 hours, turning occasionally.

Preheat oven to 375°. Arrange wings on wire rack in shallow roasting pan. Bake 40 minutes, basting occasionally with marinade, until tender, turning once. Makes 3 dozen.

Denise Love, Austell-Marietta (Dogwood Delights II)

Mushroom Pinwheels

1 (8-count) package crescent
 rolls
1 (12-ounce) can mushroom
 stems and pieces, drained

1 (8-ounce) package cream
 cheese, softened
Dash of garlic salt

Open rolls but do not divide. Leave dough in large rectangle. Mix mushrooms, cream cheese, and garlic until well blended. Spread over dough rectangle. Begin at shorter side and roll up. Cut into ½-inch slices and place on greased cookie sheet. Bake at 350° for 15–20 minutes or until lightly browned. Serve hot.

McLaughlin, Austell-Marietta (Dogwood Delights)

Stuffed Mushrooms

1 pound large mushrooms,
    cleaned, chopped
6 ounces snow crabmeat
1 cup heavy cream, divided

1 teaspoon seasoned salt
¾ cup Monterey Jack cheese,
    divided
¼ cup Italian bread crumbs

Arrange mushroom caps in shallow baking dish. Chop mushroom stems and mix with remaining ingredients, reserving ½ cup cream and ¼ cup cheese. Fill mushroom caps with spoonful of mixture. Pour reserved cream over all and sprinkle with reserved cheese. Bake at 325° for 15–20 minutes. Serve warm.

McLaughlin, Austell-Marietta (Dogwood Delights)

Zesty Stuffed Jalapeños

24 pickled jalapeños
1 (12-ounce) bag frozen peeled,
    deveined shrimp
1 medium red onion, chopped
    fine
2 cloves garlic, chopped fine

1 (8-ounce) package cream
    cheese, softened
1 lemon
Lettuce
Crackers

Cut each pepper in half and remove seeds; place in refrigerator. Cook and drain shrimp. Chop cooled shrimp finely. Mix shrimp, onion, garlic, and cream cheese together. Squeeze lemon juice over mixture and blend well. Cover and refrigerate overnight.

Fill each pepper half with shrimp mixture and serve in a bed of lettuce with crackers. Serves about 30.

Note: Do not drink water with this; it only makes your mouth hotter!

Audrey Penn, Decatur, GA (Great Southern Recipes)

Zucchini Munchies

4 eggs, well beaten
3 cups thinly sliced zucchini
½ cup sliced green onions
2 tablespoons chopped parsley
½ cup oil
½ teaspoon salt

½ teaspoon pepper
½ teaspoon garlic salt
½ cup grated Parmesan cheese
½ cup Italian seasoning
Dash of Tabasco

Combine all ingredients; mix well. Pour into lightly greased 9x13-inch pan. Bake at 350° for 25 minutes. Cut into squares. Serve warm.

Doris A. Thompson, Grayson, GA (Great Southern Recipes)

Tortilla Roll-Ups

1 (8-ounce) package cream
  cheese, softened
1 cup sour cream
1¼ cups Monterey Jack
  cheese
⅛ teaspoon garlic powder

¼ cup sliced green olives
1 (16-ounce) can black beans,
  drained
1 (8-count) package flour
  tortillas
Salsa

Mix cream cheese and sour cream till smooth. Add Monterey Jack, garlic powder, and olives. Process black beans in blender till mushy.

Spread black beans and cream cheese mixture on tortillas. Roll up tortillas individually in plastic wrap and refrigerate a few hours or overnight; slice into bite-size pieces and serve with salsa.

Jerry Farkas, Marietta, GA (Great Southern Recipes)

Delicious Deviled Eggs

1 dozen fresh eggs
2 tablespoons honey Dijon
mustard
1 tablespoon Hellmann's
mayonnaise
4 slices crisply fried bacon,
crumbled

Dash of seasoned salt
4 dashes black pepper, or to
taste
2 tablespoons sweet pickle
relish
1 teaspoon sugar

Boil eggs 10 minutes, rinse in cold water; peel while slightly warm (makes peeling easier). Slice eggs in halves and carefully remove yolks to mixing bowl. Use fork to mash yolks to smooth consistency. Add mustard and mayonnaise (may use mixer for fluffier texture). Add remaining ingredients. If needed, add a little more mayo, being careful not to add too much. You don't want the yolk mixture to be too soupy.

Place egg whites on serving tray and stuff each generously with spoonful of mixture. When all are stuffed, sprinkle each lightly with paprika. Cover tray and place into fridge till cool.

G. Moffett-Ford, Austell, GA (Great Southern Recipes)

Pineapple-Cream Cheese Sandwiches

1 (8-ounce) package cream
  cheese, softened
6 tablespoons mayonnaise
1 (15-ounce) can crushed
  pineapple, drained

½–1 cup chopped pecans
Thin-sliced wheat and white
  bread

Mix all ingredients thoroughly. Alternating white and wheat slices, make 3-layer sandwiches. Trim crusts and cut into 2, 3, or 4 sandwiches, depending on size desired.

Faye Crowe, Decatur-Tucker (Dogwood Delights)

Peppery Spiced Nuts

1 pound pecan halves
2 tablespoons butter, melted
2 teaspoons Worcestershire

Dash of hot pepper sauce
½ teaspoon salt
⅛ teaspoon pepper

Preheat oven to 325°. In a skillet, sauté pecans in butter till hot. Add remaining ingredients. Arrange nuts in shallow pan and bake at 325° for 20 minutes. Yields 4 cups.

Theresa Haddock, Brookwood-Downtown (Dogwood Delights)

Nut Nibblers

2 cups pecans or walnuts
1 egg white, beaten slightly
2 tablespoons water

½ teaspoon vanilla flavoring
⅔ cup sugar
¼ cup cornstarch

Moisten nuts with egg white, water, and vanilla. Mix sugar and cornstarch together. Toss with nuts. Spread nuts on cookie sheet. Bake 1½ hours at 250°. Stir every 15 minutes.

Gerri Christopherson, Austell-Marietta (Dogwood Delights)

Garbage

1 (12-ounce) package Rice Chex cereal
1 (16-ounce) package dry roasted peanuts
1 (12-ounce) package raisins

1 cup butter
2 cups chocolate chips
1 cup peanut butter
2 pounds powdered sugar

Mix cereal, peanuts, and raisins in large bowl. Combine butter, chocolate chips, and peanut butter in saucepan. Cook till butter and chocolate chips are melted. Pour over cereal mixture. Combine with powdered sugar in double garbage bag; toss to coat. Store in airtight containers in refrigerator. Yield 25 servings.

Judy Ellis, Athens-Gainesville Council (Lawfully Good Eating)

Bread and Breakfast

1878
Butterstamp

The first telephone with a combined receiver-transmitter that could be held in the hand looked like a butterstamp—hence its name. You talked into one end, turned the instrument around, and listened to the other end. The push button signaled the operator. This model was in service when the world's first commercial switchboard opened in New Haven, Connecticut, in 1878. Western Union opened the first large city exchange in San Francisco that same year. The public switched telephone network was born; no longer limited to people on the same wire, folks could now talk to many others on different lines.

Quick Rolls

2 cups unsifted Bisquick　　　**1 stick butter, melted**
1 cup sour cream

Mix all ingredients together.　Spoon into greased muffin pan.
Cook at 400° till lightly browned.　Makes 1 dozen.

Ruth Hood, Chamblee-North Fulton (Dogwood Delights)

Old Time Spoon Rolls

1 package dry yeast　　　　　**¼ cup sugar**
2 cups warm water　　　　　　**1 egg**
1½ sticks margarine, softened　**4 cups self-rising flour**

Dissolve yeast in water.　Cream margarine with sugar and egg.
Add yeast and water to mixture.　Mix in flour, 1 cup at a time, to
make spongy batter.　(May use electric mixer.)　Place in airtight
container and refrigerate till ready to use.

Bake in preheated 450° oven.　Place heaping tablespoon batter
into greased muffin tin.　Bake 10–15 minutes.　This mixture will
keep for a day in the refrigerator.

Susan Plaster, Austell-Marietta (Dogwood Delights II)

Angel Biscuits

5 cups self-rising flour
⅓ cup sugar
1 teaspoon baking soda
2 packages yeast, dissolved in ¼
  cup warm water

1 cup shortening
2 cups buttermilk

Mix all ingredients together till dough is formed. Cut into biscuits and bake at 425° for about 15 minutes, or till done. Dough can be kept in refrigerator for several days.

Emily Tanner, W. E.-Region (Dogwood Delights); Joyce Stuart, Chamblee-North Fulton (Dogwood Delights II)

South Georgia Egg Gravy

⅓ cup all-purpose flour
¼ cup bacon drippings

3 eggs, beaten
Milk

Stir flour into bacon drippings in large heavy skillet till smooth. Cook till golden brown, stirring constantly. Add eggs and enough milk to make of desired consistency. Cook till thickened, stirring constantly. Serve over hot biscuits. Yields 4 servings.

Bill House, Sheriff of Stewart County (Lawfully Good Eating)

Low-Fat Biscuits

2 cups self-rising flour
½ cup skim milk

¼ cup canola oil

Preheat oven to 450°. Measure flour into bowl and make a hole or "well" in middle. Pour milk into well and pour oil on top. Gently blend till flour is moist. Add more milk if needed to mix in all the flour. Add more flour if too wet. Dough will come away from sides of bowl and form ball. Handle as little as possible.

Roll out to about ½ inch between 2 sheets of wax paper. Cut into rounds, and bake on ungreased cookie sheet. Makes about a dozen medium-size biscuits. You can also drop by spoonfuls or shape by hand.

Phyllis Yancey, Decatur, GA (Great Southern Recipes)

Cheese Biscuits

2 cups baking mix
½–¾ cup shredded Cheddar
cheese

1 cup sour cream
Melted butter

Combine baking mix, cheese, and sour cream in bowl; mix well. Drop by spoonfuls onto greased baking sheet. Bake at 425° for 10 minutes, or till golden brown. Brush tops with butter. May add garlic to butter, if desired. Yields 1½ dozen.

Ann Pollard, Columbus Council (Lawfully Good Eating)

Old Bob's Better Than Grandma's Biscuits

1 (¼-ounce) package RapidRise yeast	2 tablespoons sugar
	½ teaspoon lemon juice
4 ounces mildly hot water	1 cup milk
⅛ teaspoon baking powder	6 level tablespoons Crisco
4 cups self-rising flour, divided	shortening

Preheat oven to 400°. Dissolve yeast in water; do not stir; set aside. Mix baking powder with flour, sifting twice; set aside. Mix sugar, yeast mixture, and lemon juice with milk.

Blend Crisco into 3¾ cups flour using a wire blend tool or fork, but be sure it is well blended. Dust bread board or mixing surface with remaining ¼ cup flour. Add milk mixture to flour; mix well with spoon till mixture pulls away from mixing bowl sides. Place dough on floured surface and knead with hands no more than 5 times. (Too much kneading will cause dough to toughen.) Roll out dough to ¾-inch thickness and cut with biscuit cutter. Or roll dough with hands into golf-ball size balls and flatten slightly. Lightly grease a 10x20-inch bread pan. Place biscuits in prepared pan, allowing approximately ½ inch between each. Bake biscuits until slightly browned (about 15 minutes); remove from oven, butter to taste, and enjoy. Yields 16–20 biscuits.

Bob Kelley, Area (Dogwood Delights II)

Sweet Potato Biscuits

¾ cup cold mashed sweet
  potato
4 tablespoons butter, melted
⅔ cup milk

½ cup sugar
½ teaspoon salt
2 cups all-purpose flour
4 teaspoons baking powder

Blend sweet potato, butter, and milk together. Sift dry ingredients together. Mix together well, and drop by spoonful onto a greased cookie sheet. Bake 12–15 minutes at 450°, until peaks start to turn brown. Serve warm with butter. Freezes well.

JoAnne Snedeker, Alpharetta, GA (Great Southern Recipes)

Hush Puppies

1½ cups self-rising, bolted
  white cornmeal
1 cup self-rising flour
1 tablespoon sugar
¼ teaspoon salt

½ teaspoon onion powder
1 cup chopped onion
1 teaspoon peanut oil
1 whole egg
1 cup buttermilk

Combine dry ingredients. Mix all wet ingredients and add to dry ingredients. Let rise ½ hour. Spoon into 375° deep fat. Cook to a golden brown; drain and serve. Yields approximately 30 hush puppies.

Editor's Extra: Bolted cornmeal is a finely ground meal; you may use regular self-rising cornmeal.

Jerry Witt, General; Lola Daniel, W.E.-Service/Installation; Sara Fields, Columbus Life Member Club (Dogwood Delights)

Fresh Hot Water Cornbread

2 cups self-rising white
   cornmeal
2 tablespoons all-purpose flour
1 large egg

2 tablespoons sugar
1½ cups hot water
Oil

Combine cornmeal, flour, egg, sugar, and hot water; mix well. Pour enough oil into medium skillet to cover bottom. Heat till hot. Place about 2 heaping tablespoons mixture for each bread patty in skillet. Fry in hot oil over medium heat till edges are light brown. Flip and fry till bottom is light brown. Add more oil, as needed, to fry patties in batches. Drain on paper towels.

Lavonia Brewer, Lithonia, GA (Great Southern Recipes)

Cornbread Muffins

1 cup self-rising cornmeal mix
1 cup self-rising flour
1¼–1½ cups milk or
   buttermilk

¼ cup oil
1 large egg, lightly beaten
1 teaspoon sugar (optional)

Preheat oven to 425°. Spray muffin tin with Pam or Baker's Joy. Mix all ingredients together and stir till batter is no longer lumpy. Pour mixture into muffin tin; will make 12 muffins. Bake for approximately 20–25 minutes or till muffins are brown. Remove from tin and serve hot.

Dorothy Fulcher, Decatur, GA (Great Southern Recipes)

German Cornbread

1½ cups self-rising cornmeal
2 eggs
½ cup oil
1 (8-ounce) can cream-style
  corn, or fresh corn

1 cup sour cream
1 large onion, chopped

Mix all ingredients together. Grease heavy skillet and sprinkle with cornmeal. Heat skillet, then pour in mixture. Bake at 400° for 30–35 minutes or till brown.

Jean Bracey, General (Dogwood Delights)

Spinach Corn Muffins

1 (10-ounce) package frozen
  chopped spinach
2 boxes Jiffy corn muffin mix

2 eggs
⅔ cup milk

Preheat oven to 400°. Cook spinach according to package directions; drain. Blend muffin mix, eggs, and milk. Add drained spinach to mix. Spray 12 muffin tins with Pam. Fill tins ⅔ full. Bake 20–25 minutes or till brown on top.

Susan Sloan, Fayetteville, GA (Great Southern Recipes)

Cheese and Bacon Muffins

1 egg
2 tablespoons oil or melted
   shortening
¾ cup milk

1 cup self-rising cornmeal
1 teaspoon sugar
4 strips bacon, cooked, crumbled
½ cup grated Cheddar cheese

Heat oven to 450°. Grease and heat skillet, muffin pans, or corn stick molds. Beat egg in mixing bowl; add remaining ingredients and stir until well blended. Pour into pan. Bake 18–20 minutes for skillet, 15–28 minutes for muffins or sticks.

Magnolia Pugh, W. E.-Service/Installation (Dogwood Delights)

Raisin Bran Muffins

2 cups All-Bran Cereal
2 cups boiling water
1 cup shortening
3 cups sugar
4 eggs
1 quart buttermilk

3 cups all-purpose flour
1 tablespoon salt
3 tablespoons baking soda
4 cups bran flakes
2 cups raisins

Mix cereal and boiling water together; set aside. Cream shortening and sugar; add eggs, buttermilk, and cereal mixture. Sift flour, salt, and baking soda and add to mixture. Add bran flakes and mix until moist. Add raisins. Put in refrigerator for a day. Mixture will keep for 6 weeks. Bake in muffin tins at 375° for 20–25 minutes.

Gerri Christopherson, Austell-Marietta (Dogwood Delights)

Breakfast Sausage Muffins

1 pound sausage
5–6 canned biscuits
2 eggs

1 (3-ounce) package cream
    cheese, softened
Shredded Cheddar cheese

Preheat oven to 375°. Brown sausage; drain; set aside. Flatten each biscuit with a rolling pin and line greased muffin tin with each biscuit.

In a blender, combine eggs and cream cheese. Fill each muffin evenly with egg mixture. Spoon sausage evenly into each muffin. Top each with Cheddar cheese. Bake till golden brown.

Lynn Martin, Douglasville, GA (Great Southern Recipes)

Poppy Seed Bread

BREAD:

3 eggs, beaten
1⅛ cups oil
3 cups all-purpose flour
2¼ cups sugar
1½ cups milk
1½ teaspoons salt

1½ teaspoons baking powder
1½ teaspoons vanilla
1½ teaspoons almond extract
1½ teaspoons butter extract
1½ tablespoons poppy seeds

Mix all ingredients well. Pour into 2 greased 5x9-inch loaf pans and bake at 350° for 1 hour.

GLAZE:

1½ teaspoons butter extract
1½ teaspoons almond extract
1½ teaspoons vanilla extract

¼ cup orange juice
¾ cup sugar

Combine all ingredients and pour over warm bread.

Janet Tallent, General (Dogwood Delights)

Cherry Bread

1 cup sugar
2 eggs
1 teaspoon salt
1½ cups all-purpose flour

½ cup chopped nuts
1 (4½-ounce) jar maraschino
cherries, cut up with juice

Mix all ingredients together. Bake in 2 small 4x8-inch greased loaf pans in 325° oven 50 minutes.

Gerri Christopherson, Austell-Marietta (Dogwood Delights)

Date Nut Bread

½ cup oil
1 cup sugar
4 eggs

1 cup self-rising flour
1 quart chopped pecans
1 package sugar-coated dates

Cream oil and sugar; add beaten eggs, flour, pecans, and dates. Line loaf pan with wax paper; pour dough in and put into cold oven. Bake at 300° for 2 hours. Cool on rack.

Wilma Presnell, Chamblee-North Fulton (Dogwood Delights)

Excellent Zucchini Bread

3 eggs
1 cup oil
2 cups sugar
2 teaspoons vanilla
3 cups all-purpose flour
2 teaspoons baking soda
¼ teaspoon baking powder
1 teaspoon salt

1½ teaspoons cinnamon
¾ teaspoon nutmeg
1 (8¼-ounce) can crushed
   pineapple, well drained
1 cup chopped pecans
2 cups shredded, unpeeled
   zucchini
1 cup chopped dates

Beat eggs, oil, sugar, and vanilla until thick. Stir in remaining ingredients. Pour into 2 greased 9x5-inch loaf pans. Bake about 1 hour in preheated 350° oven.

Marilyn Jeffries, General (Dogwood Delights)

Hawaiian Bread

3 cups all-purpose flour
2 cups sugar
1 teaspoon cinnamon
1 teaspoon salt
1 teaspoon baking soda
1 cup chopped nuts

3 eggs, beaten
1½ cups oil
2 cup mashed bananas
1 (8-ounce) can crushed
   pineapple, drained
2 teaspoons vanilla

Combine all ingredients, mixing well. Pour into greased 5x9-inch loaf pan and bake at 350° for 1 hour and 15 minutes.

Sue Storey, Decatur-Tucker (Dogwood Delights II)

Lemon Tea Bread

½ cup milk
2 eggs
1 cup sugar
⅓ cup margarine, melted
1½ teaspoons grated lemon peel

1¼ cups all-purpose flour
1 teaspoon double-acting baking powder
1 teaspoon salt
½ cup chopped pecans

GLAZE:

¼ cup sugar

3 tablespoons fresh lemon juice

Preheat oven to 350°. Grease an 4½x8½-inch loaf pan; set aside. In large mixer bowl, combine milk, eggs, sugar, margarine, and lemon peel. Beat at medium speed until well blended. Add dry ingredients; beat at low speed just till they are moistened and mixture is smooth. Fold in pecans. Pour into loaf pan. Bake 45–50 minutes or till toothpick inserted in center comes out clean.

Meanwhile, combine sugar and lemon juice for Glaze. Place bread, still in pan, on wire rack to cool. Slowly pour on Glaze while bread is still hot. Let stand 10 minutes in pan; remove bread and cool completely on wire rack.

Debbie Quakenbush, W. E.-BLT/Cable (Dogwood Delights)

Moist Banana-Nut Bread

1 cup margarine, softened	½ cup buttermilk
2½ cups sugar	3 teaspoons vanilla, divided
4 eggs	4 or 5 bananas, chopped
3 cups all-purpose flour	Powdered sugar
1 teaspoon baking soda	

Cream margarine and sugar in mixer bowl till light and fluffy. Beat in eggs. Add flour, baking soda, buttermilk, 2 teaspoons vanilla, and bananas; mix well. Spoon into 2 greased and floured 5x9-inch loaf pans. Bake at 350° for 1 hour or till loaves test done. Remove to wire rack. Combine powdered sugar and remaining 1 teaspoon vanilla with enough water to make a thin icing in bowl; mix well. Spread over warm loaves. Yields 24 servings.

Sara Tadlock, Augusta Council (Lawfully Good Eating)

Pumpkin Bread

3 cups sugar	1 teaspoon cloves
1 cup Wesson oil	1 teaspoon cinnamon
4 eggs	2 teaspoons salt
2 cups pumpkin	1 teaspoon baking powder
⅔ cup water	1 teaspoon nutmeg
3½ cups all-purpose flour	1 teaspoon allspice
2 teaspoons baking soda	

Cream together the sugar and oil. Add eggs, mixing well. Mix in pumpkin. Stir dry ingredients together. Add alternately to mixture along with water. Pour into 4 well-greased and floured loaf pans. Bake at 350° for 50–60 minutes. If using mini loaf pans, bake for 35 minutes.

Jeanne Samoray, General (Dogwood Delights); Irene Mooney, Chamblee-North Fulton (Dogwood Delights II)

Pimento Cheese Loaf

12 slices sandwich bread
2 cups hot water
1 stick butter, melted
1 (12-ounce) can evaporated
  milk
1 (4-ounce) jar pimentos with
  juice, grated or mashed

¾ pound sharp Cheddar cheese,
  grated
½ teaspoon salt
3 eggs, slightly beaten

Break bread in pan; pour hot water over and mash. Add butter, milk, pimento, cheese, salt, and eggs. Mix thoroughly. Bake at 375°–400° for 25–30 minutes or until brown. Serves 8–10.

Mrs. Glenn Hatcher, General (Dogwood Delights)

Cheese Onion Bread

½ cup chopped onion
3 tablespoons butter, melted,
  divided
1 egg, beaten

½ cup milk
1½ cups Bisquick
1 cup grated Cheddar cheese,
  divided

Cook onion in 1 tablespoon butter till tender, but not brown. Combine egg and milk. Add Bisquick and stir till mixed. Add onion and ½ cup cheese. Place in greased 5x9-inch loaf pan. Top with remaining cheese and melted butter. Bake at 350° for 30 minutes.

Shirley Clary, Decatur-Tucker (Dogwood Delights II)

Funnel Cakes

2 eggs
⅔ cup milk
1⅓ cups all-purpose flour
2 tablespoons sugar

1 teaspoon baking powder
¼ teaspoon salt
Oil for frying
Powdered sugar

Beat eggs and milk in bowl. Sift flour, sugar, baking powder, and salt together. Add to egg mixture; mix well. Heat 2 inches oil in 4-quart saucepan. Fill funnel half full with batter, holding finger over spout. Drizzle batter in spiral into hot oil. Fry till golden brown, turning once; drain. Sprinkle with powdered sugar. Yields 6 servings.

Millie Malloy, Athens-Gainesville Council
(Lawfully Good Eating)

Quick Monkey Bread

½ cup chopped pecans
½ cup sugar
1 teaspoon ground cinnamon
3 (10-ounce) cans refrigerated
   buttermilk biscuits

1 cup firmly packed brown
   sugar
½ cup butter or margarine,
   melted

Sprinkle chopped pecans evenly in bottom of a well-greased 10-inch Bundt pan; set aside. Combine sugar and cinnamon. Cut biscuits into quarters; roll each piece in sugar mixture and layer in pan. Combine brown sugar and butter; pour over dough. Bake at 350° for 30–40 minutes. Cool bread 10 minutes in pan; invert onto serving platter.

Joan Cole, Chamblee-North Fulton (Dogwood Delights)

Brunch Pull-Apart Bread

¼ cup grated Parmesan cheese
3 tablespoons sesame seeds
½ teaspoon crushed dried
  basil
1 (24-count) package frozen
  unbaked rolls

¼ cup butter, melted
2 tablespoons bacon bites
  (optional)

Grease 10-inch fluted tube pan. Mix Parmesan cheese, sesame seeds, and basil. Add ⅓ of mixture to greased pan, coating sides and bottom. Place 10 frozen rolls in pan; drizzle with half the butter. Sprinkle half of remaining cheese mixture on top. Add remaining rolls. Drizzle with remaining butter and cheese mixture. Cover and let rolls thaw and rise (12–24 hours) in refrigerator.

Let stand at room temperature 30 minutes. Bake, uncovered, in 350° oven 20 minutes. Cover with foil and bake 10–15 minutes till golden. Cool on wire rack. Serve warm. Makes 12 servings.

Toni Cook, General (Dogwood Delights II)

Raw Apple Coffee Cake

½ cup shortening
1 cup sugar
1 egg
1 cup all-purpose flour
1 teaspoon baking soda

¼ teaspoon salt
1 teaspoon vanilla
2 cups diced tart apples
½ cup chopped nuts
½ cup plump raisins

Mix shortening, sugar, egg, flour, baking soda, salt, and vanilla. Add apples, nuts, and raisins; blend well. Pour into greased and floured 8-inch-square pan. Bake in 350° oven for 45 minutes.

Brownie Scott, Marietta, GA (Great Southern Recipes)

Coffee Cake

FILLING:

1 cup brown sugar
3 tablespoons all-purpose flour
4 tablespoons butter, melted

1 tablespoon cinnamon
1 cup chopped nuts

Mix all ingredients well; set aside.

BATTER:

3 cups all-purpose flour
6 teaspoons baking powder
1 teaspoon salt
1¼ cups sugar
1 stick butter, softened

2 eggs
1 cup milk
1½ teaspoons vanilla
¼ teaspoon cinnamon
¼ teaspoon nutmeg

Sift flour, baking powder, salt, and sugar. Cut in butter until like fine cornmeal. Blend in well-beaten eggs, milk, vanilla, cinnamon, and nutmeg. Grease 9x13-inch baking pan. Pour in and spread ½ Batter; put in ½ of Filling, then rest of Batter. Top with rest of Filling. Bake in 350° oven 30–35 minutes. When toothpick comes out clean, it's done.

Pat Bates, General (Dogwood Delights)

Orange-Cinnamon Rolls

2 (8-ounce) cans refrigerated
    crescent rolls
3 tablespoons orange juice
2 tablespoons butter, softened
½ cup firmly packed brown
    sugar

¼ cup chopped pecans
¼ cup sugar
1 tablespoon ground cinnamon

Unroll crescent rolls and press perforations together to form 2 long rectangles. Stir together orange juice, butter, brown sugar, pecans, sugar, and cinnamon. Spread evenly over each rectangle. Roll up jellyroll fashion and cut each log into 1-inch-wide slices.

Place rolls ¼ inch apart on 2 greased 8-inch cake pans. Bake at 375° for 15–18 minutes, or till golden. Cool 5–10 minutes. Drizzle with Glaze. Makes 2 dozen.

GLAZE:
⅔ cup powdered sugar
1 teaspoon milk
1 teaspoon orange juice

¼ teaspoon vanilla
⅛ teaspoon salt

Stir ingredients together well. Drizzle over warm rolls.

Doris Thompson, Grayson, GA (Great Southern Recipes)

Maple Bacon Oven Pancakes

1½ cups Bisquick
1 tablespoon sugar
2 eggs
¾ cup milk
¼ cup maple syrup

1½ cups shredded Cheddar
cheese, divided
12 slices bacon, fried crisp,
crumbled

Heat oven to 425°. Grease and flour 9x13-inch pan. Beat Bisquick, sugar, eggs, milk, and syrup with ½ cup cheese with hand beater till smooth. Pour into pan. Bake uncovered till wooden pick comes out clean (10–15 minutes). Sprinkle with remaining cheese and bacon. Bake uncovered till cheese is melted (3–5 minutes). Serve with warm syrup and/or jelly.

Anne E. Kaiser, W. E.-BLT/Cable (Dogwood Delights)

World's Best Pancakes

2 cups self-rising flour
2 tablespoons sugar
2 cups milk

2 large eggs
2 tablespoons oil

Measure flour and sugar into sifter and sift into mixing bowl. Separate eggs and beat whites till stiff. Beat yolks and milk till mixed. Make a well in center of flour, pour in milk and mix just till lumps are gone. Add egg whites and mix just a little. Add oil and mix just a little more. Bake on 425° griddle, turning when bubbles form all over pancake and edges appear dry. Makes about 36 (4-inch) pancakes. Chopped nuts may be added to batter before egg whites.

Jack Horton, General (Dogwood Delights)

Baked Peach Pancake

2 cups fresh or frozen sliced,
  peeled peaches
4 teaspoons sugar
1 teaspoon lemon juice
3 eggs
½ cup all-purpose flour

½ cup milk
½ teaspoon salt
2 tablespoons butter or
  margarine
Ground nutmeg
Sour cream (optional)

Combine peaches, sugar, and lemon juice; set aside. In mixing bowl, beat eggs till fluffy. Add flour, milk, and salt; beat till smooth. Place butter in a 10-inch skillet; bake at 400° for 3–5 minutes till melted.

Immediately pour batter into hot skillet. Bake 20–25 minutes or till pancake has risen and is puffed all over. Fill with peach slices and sprinkle with nutmeg. Serve immediately with sour cream, if desired. Serves 4–6.

Teresa L. Roberts, Conyers, GA (Great Southern Recipes)

Buttermilk Pecan Waffles

2 cups all-purpose flour
1 tablespoon baking powder
1 teaspoon baking soda
½ teaspoon salt

4 eggs
2 cups buttermilk
½ cup butter, melted
3 tablespoons chopped pecans

Combine flour, baking powder, baking soda, and salt; set aside. Beat eggs till light and fluffy; add buttermilk, and mix well. Add dry ingredients and beat till batter is smooth. Stir in butter.

Pour about ¾ cup batter onto a lightly greased preheated waffle iron. Sprinkle with a few pecans. Bake till golden brown. Repeat till batter and pecans are gone. Makes 7 (8-inch) waffles.

Teresa L. Roberts, Conyers, GA (Great Southern Recipes);
Barbara West, W.E.-Region (Dogwood Delights)

Cheese Soufflé

A great brunch, lunch, supper, or anytime treat.

2 tablespoons margarine	1 cup grated cheese
1 tablespoon flour	4 eggs, separated
1½ cups milk	

Melt margarine slowly. Add flour, blending as added. Add milk, stirring constantly. While hot, add cheese and stir till melted. Allow to cool (but not cold). Beat egg yolks, then whites till peaks form. Add beaten yolks to mixture, then fold in whites. Pour mixture into buttered casserole. Bake, putting casserole in pan of water, in 350° oven till straw will not stick, 30–35 minutes. Serve hot. Serves 4.

Mrs. R. K. Babington, General (Dogwood Delights)

Brunch Casserole

8 slices white bread	4 eggs, beaten
½ pound grated Cheddar cheese	2 cups milk
	½ teaspoon salt
1 pound sausage, cooked, crumbled	Dash of pepper
	1 teaspoon dry mustard

Grease an 8x12-inch baking dish. Place bread as a liner in bottom of dish; sprinkle with cheese, then sausage. Mix eggs, milk, salt, pepper, and mustard. Pour over sausage and cheese. Refrigerate overnight.

The next day, bake at 350° for 30–35 minutes till eggs are set. Serves 6–8.

Marcia Davenport, Austell-Marietta (Dogwood Delights)

Grits Casserole

1 cup uncooked grits
1 stick butter
4 ounces Cheez Whiz
⅔ cup milk

3 eggs, well beaten
4 slices bacon, fried, crumbled
Salt and pepper to taste
½ cup grated Cheddar cheese

Cook grits according to instructions on box. Add butter and Cheez Whiz; stir till melted. Cool slightly. Mix milk and eggs and add to grits. Add bacon. Pour into greased 2-quart casserole. Sprinkle with grated cheese. Bake in 350° oven 45 minutes. Serves 6.

Lucy Smith, Austell-Marietta (Dogwood Delights)

Brunch Casserole

1 (8-count) can crescent rolls
8 ounces shaved ham
2 cups shredded mozzarella
  cheese
2 cups shredded sharp Cheddar
  cheese

8 eggs (or equivalent egg
  substitute)
1 cup skim milk

Preheat oven to 425°. Line buttered 9x13-inch pan with rolls, pressing to close perforations. Layer ham, mozzarella, and Cheddar. Beat eggs with milk. Pour over casserole. Bake 30–40 minutes at 425°. Let cool 10 minutes before serving.

Susan Sloan, Fayetteville, GA (Great Southern Recipes)

Breakfast Casserole

6 eggs
1 cup milk
1 (32-ounce) bag O'Brien
  potatoes

1 pound sausage cooked,
  crumbled
1 pound Velveeta cheese, diced

Beat together eggs and milk. Combine all ingredients; mix well.
Pour into greased 9x13-inch casserole dish. Bake, uncovered, 1
hour at 375°.

Mandy Fridge, Atlanta, GA (Great Southern Recipes)

Breakfast Quiche

1½ cups cheese, cubed or
  shredded
Sausage, bacon, ham, turkey,
  or ground beef, browned,
  drained
½ cup chopped onion
1 (9-inch) deep-dish pie shell

4–6 eggs, beaten
¾ cup heavy whipping cream
Salt and pepper to taste
Optional ingredients: ¼ cup
  chopped: green pepper, yellow
  pepper, red pepper, orange
  pepper, mushrooms

Mix cheese, meat, and onion together and place in pie shell. Beat
eggs and cream till light and fluffy. Season to taste. Pour over
ingredients in shell and bake at 350° till firm and crust is brown. If
you want the pie to be cheesier, add a total of 2 cups shredded
cheese.

Lavonia Brewer, Lithonia, GA (Great Southern Recipes)

The "Real Men Do Eat Quiche" Quiche

1½ cups shredded cheese
2 tablespoons all-purpose flour
2 eggs
1 cup milk
Salt and pepper to taste

Chopped, cooked ham
Chopped, cooked broccoli
1 unbaked 9- or 10-inch pie
   shell

Toss cheese with flour; set aside. Beat eggs with milk, salt and pepper in small bowl; set aside. Layer ham and broccoli in pastry-lined quiche pan. Sprinkle with cheese; pour in egg mixture. Bake at 400° for 40 minutes, or till knife inserted near center comes out clean. Yields 6 servings.

Marie Driver, Athens-Gainesville Council
(Lawfully Good Eating)

Hash Brown Quiche

3 cups frozen loose-pack
  shredded hash browns,
  thawed
⅓ cup butter or margarine,
  melted
1 cup diced fully cooked ham

1 cup shredded Cheddar cheese
¼ cup diced green bell pepper
2 eggs
½ cup milk
½ teaspoon salt
¼ teaspoon pepper

Press hash browns between paper towels to remove excess moisture. Press into bottom and up sides of ungreased 9-inch pie plate. Drizzle with butter. Bake at 425° for 25 minutes.

Combine ham, cheese, and green pepper; spoon over crust. In a small bowl, beat eggs, milk, salt, and pepper. Pour over all. Reduce heat to 350°; bake 25–30 minutes, or till knife inserted near center comes out clean. Allow to stand 10 minutes before cutting. Serves 6.

Teresa L. Roberts, Conyers, GA (Great Southern Recipes)

The Bridle Path Breakfast Casserole

4 cups thinly sliced potatoes
1 pound spicy sausage, cooked,
  crumbled, drained
2 cups shredded Swiss cheese,
  divided

2 cups cubed ham
6 eggs
¼ teaspoon dry mustard
Salt and pepper to taste
1 cup milk

Layer potatoes in buttered baking dish. Top with sausage, 1 cup cheese, and ham. Beat eggs with mustard, salt, pepper, and milk. Pour over top layer. Sprinkle with remaining cheese. Bake at 350° for 45 minutes. Serve with toast or banana bread. Serves 6–8 .

Karen J. Taylor, Athens Council (Lawfully Good Eating)

Never Fail Dumplings

2 cups all-purpose flour
4 teaspoons baking powder
½ teaspoon salt

1 tablespoon shortening
1 cup milk
1 egg, beaten

Sift flour, baking powder, and salt; cut in shortening. Stir in milk and egg. Dough should hold up the spoon. Drop in gravy or broth and cook at a simmer, covered, for about 20 minutes.

Gloria Borstelmann, Area (Dogwood Delights II)

Cornbread Dressing

1 skillet cornbread
6 cold biscuits
1 (16-ounce) package Pepperidge
   Farm cornbread stuffing
1 cup finely chopped celery
1 cup finely chopped onion
3 eggs

1 (10¾-ounce) can cream of
   celery soup (optional)
1 cup broth from cooked turkey
   (optional)
3 or 4 (14-ounce) cans chicken
   broth

Preheat oven to 425°. Crumble cornbread and biscuits into large bowl; add stuffing, celery, onion, eggs, and soup, if desired. Add broth from turkey, if using, and begin mixing with hands. Gradually add chicken broth, mixing until dressing has desired consistency. (It should make a plopping sound when slapped.)

Put dressing in 2 greased 9x13-inch glass casserole dishes. Bake 30 minutes at 425° or till it starts to brown. (Or bake one now, save one for later. Can be frozen.)

Susan Sloan, Fayetteville, GA (Great Southern Recipes)

Chicken Dressing

½ medium onion, chopped
2 sticks celery, chopped
3 cups hot water
3 chicken bouillon cubes
1 stick butter

1 egg
1 package herb-seasoned
    stuffing mix
1 tablespoon sage

Cook onion and celery until almost done in water with bouillon cubes and butter; set aside. Beat egg and add to dry stuffing mix. Stir well and add sage. Mix all ingredients well. Bake in greased pan at 350° for 45 minutes or till golden brown on top.

Mary Townsend, Chamblee-North Fulton (Dogwood Delights)

Soups, Stews, and Chilies

1882
Three-Box

This oak-encased instrument was the standard for many years and one of the first to place the crank more conveniently on the side. The top box contained a ringer and a switchhook. The middle box was a Blake transmitter, which was known for its improved voice clarity. The bottom, a cover for a wet cell battery, doubled as a writing shelf. To place a call, you turned the crank to ring the operator, then picked up the receiver. The operator would then answer and connect you to the party you wished to call. To signal the operator to disconnect the call, you would hang up the receiver and turn the crank to produce a short ring. This was called "ringing off."

Chicken Soup

1 (2- to 3-pound) chicken
1 onion, chopped
Salt and pepper to taste
4–6 potatoes, peeled, cubed
2 chicken bouillon cubes

1 (10¾-ounce) can cream of
  mushroom soup
2 (12-ounce) cans evaporated
  milk
Flour

Cook chicken with onion, salt and pepper in water to cover in stockpot till chicken is tender. Remove chicken, reserving broth; discard skin and bones. Cook potatoes in reserved broth with bouillon cubes till tender, stirring occasionally. Add chicken and mushroom soup. Cook 5 minutes. Add evaporated milk and enough flour to thicken slightly; mix well. Cook till heated through, but do not boil. Yields 6–8 servings.

Diane McHargue, Augusta Council (Lawfully Good Eating)

Chicken Soup

4 large boneless chicken
  breasts
1 tablespoon oil
1½ cups rice
3 medium potatoes, peeled,
  cubed
3 medium carrots, sliced
2 medium onions (whole)

5 cups water
1 cup tomato sauce
Onion powder to taste
Garlic powder to taste
Salt and pepper to taste
Thyme, basil, parsley to taste
Pinch of oregano

Chop chicken and brown in oil in Dutch oven. Add remaining ingredients; cook covered till done (30–45 minutes).

Sally T. Beckett, W.E.-Service/Installations (Dogwood Delights)

Homemade Soup

1 pound short ribs, cut into
  serving pieces
Salt to taste
6 large potatoes, peeled, cubed
1 (10-ounce) package frozen
  corn
1 (14½-ounce) can tomatoes

1 (10-ounce) package frozen
  black-eyed peas or field peas
1 (10-ounce) package frozen
  baby lima beans
1 (8-ounce) can tomato sauce
1 cup raw rice

Place ribs in boiling water to cover with salt. Cook 1 hour, or till ribs are tender. Add potatoes, corn, tomatoes, peas, limas, tomato sauce, and rice; mix well. Cook over medium heat 1 hour, stirring frequently. Yields 6–10 servings.

Tommy Bass, Decatur County Sheriff's Department
(Lawfully Good Eating)

Steak Soup

1 stick margarine
1 cup all-purpose flour
½ gallon water
1½ pounds ground chuck
1 cup chopped onion
1 cup chopped carrots

2 cups frozen mixed vegetables
1 (14½-ounce) can tomatoes
1 tablespoon Ac'cent
2 tablespoons beef base
1 teaspoon black pepper

Melt margarine in saucepan. Whisk in flour to make a smooth paste. Stir in water. Sauté ground chuck; drain; add to saucepan. Parboil onion and carrots; add to mix. Add remaining ingredients and bring to a boil. Reduce heat; simmer till vegetables are done. Do not salt.

Margaret Patrick, Long Lines-AT&T Communications
(Dogwood Delights)

Hearty Beef and Vegetable Soup

½ pound lean ground beef
1 medium onion, chopped
2 (16-ounce) cans stewed
   tomatoes
1 (15-ounce) can red kidney
   beans or pinto beans
2 medium carrots, sliced or
   1 (16-ounce) can sliced carrots

½ head (medium) cabbage,
   cut into chunks
½ cup macaroni
3 cans chicken broth (fat on top
   removed)
2 cans water
Dash of salt and pepper (to
   taste)

Brown beef and onion in large pot. Stir in all other ingredients. Cook over medium heat until macaroni and vegetables are soft (30 minutes). If canned carrots are used, add just before other vegetables are done.

Betty McDilda, Central (Dogwood Delights II)

Santa Fe Soup

2 pounds ground chuck
1 onion, chopped
2 packages taco seasoning mix
2 packages ranch dry dressing
   mix
2 (14½-ounce) cans diced
   tomatoes
1 (15-ounce) can black beans

1 (15-ounce) can pinto beans
1 (15-ounce) can kidney beans
2 (14-ounce) cans shoepeg corn
   (or Mexicorn)
4 cups water
Sour cream for garnish
Grated cheese for garnish

Brown ground chuck and onion together; drain. Add remaining ingredients and simmer up to 2 hours. When serving, garnish with sour cream and/or cheese.

Note: May substitute chopped cooked chicken for chuck.

Brenda Harris, Loganville, GA (Great Southern Recipes)

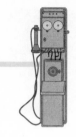

Tortilla Soup

4 tablespoons butter
½ cup oil
1 large onion, chopped
1 jalapeño, seeded, chopped
4 garlic cloves, minced
2 large carrots, diced
6 ribs celery, diced
1 pound uncooked chicken,
   boned, diced
1 teaspoon each: ground cumin,
   chili powder, salt, lemon
   pepper

3 teaspoons Tabasco
½ cup all-purpose flour
1 (14½-ounce) can tomatoes
1 (10½-ounce) can chicken broth
   or stock
8 corn tortillas, cut in strips
1 cup sour cream for garnish
3 avocados, diced for garnish
1 cup grated Cheddar cheese for
   garnish

Heat butter and oil in large kettle and sauté onion, jalapeño, garlic, carrots, celery, and chicken; simmer 5 minutes. Combine with cumin, chili powder, salt, lemon pepper, Tabasco, and flour. Add tomatoes and chicken broth; simmer 1 hour.

Drop tortilla strips into oil or melted shortening heated to 375° and fry till crisp; drain on paper towels. Put a few tortilla strips in bottom of 6–8 soup cups and add a spoon each of sour cream, avocado, and cheese. Top with soup. Serves 6–8.

Bill Kent (Great Southern Recipes)

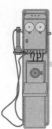

Taco Soup

1 pound ground beef
1 large onion, chopped
3 (16-ounce) cans chili beans, undrained
1 (10-ounce) can Ro-Tel
1 (15-ounce) can whole-kernel corn, undrained
1 (14½ -ounce) can chopped tomatoes
1 (8-ounce) can tomato sauce
1 package taco seasoning mix
1 package ranch seasoning dressing mix

Brown ground beef with onion; drain well. In large pot, combine ground beef, onion, and remaining ingredients; bring to a boil. Simmer 15–20 minutes. Serve with Toppings of your choice.

TOPPINGS:
Tortilla chips
Shredded cheese
Shredded lettuce
Chopped avocado
Chopped tomatoes
Sour cream

Em Posey (Great Southern Recipes)

Bulldog Bean Soup

8–16 ounces dried beans
2 tablespoons salt
2 quarts water
2 ham hocks or chopped ham
1 onion, chopped
1 (28-ounce) can tomatoes
1 red pepper, chopped, or
1 teaspoon chili powder
Juice of 1 lemon
Salt and pepper to taste

Soak beans in water to cover with 2 tablespoons salt overnight; drain. Add 2 quarts water and ham hocks. Bring to a boil; reduce heat; simmer 3 hours, stirring occasionally. Add onion, tomatoes, red pepper, lemon juice, salt and pepper; mix well. Simmer 1 hour longer. Yields 6–12 servings.

Amber Jaynes, Athens-Gainesville Council
(Lawfully Good Eating)

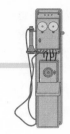

Tuscan Bean Soup

8 ounces dried Great Northern
  beans
8 ounces dried pinto beans
1½ cups chopped ham
2 leeks, thinly sliced
2 stalks celery, finely chopped
1 onion, chopped
2 cloves garlic, finely chopped
3 tablespoons olive oil
½ teaspoon dried crushed
  rosemary

¼ teaspoon red pepper
9 cups beef broth
1 (14½-ounce) can whole
  tomatoes, chopped
2 zucchini, cut into ½-inch
  cubes
13 (½-inch-thick) slices Italian
  bread
Olive oil
Freshly grated Parmesan
  cheese

Soak beans in water to cover overnight; drain and set aside. Sauté ham, leeks, celery, onion, and garlic in olive oil in large saucepan over medium heat 5 minutes. Add beans, rosemary, red pepper, beef broth, and chopped undrained tomatoes; mix well. Bring to a boil; reduce heat to medium. Simmer, partially covered, 2 hours or till beans are tender, stirring occasionally.

  Stir in zucchini. Simmer, covered, 30 minutes longer. Brush bread slices with olive oil; place on baking sheet. Bake at 375° till toasted on both sides. Ladle soup into heated serving bowls. Float toast in each bowl; sprinkle with Parmesan cheese. Yields 13 servings.

Margaret Casalino, Augusta Council (Lawfully Good Eating)

Easy Italian Wedding Soup

MEATBALLS:

1¾ pounds lean ground beef
¼ pound ground pork
½ cup bread crumbs

½ cup grated Romano cheese
Salt, pepper, and garlic powder
to taste

Combine ingredients well; make into small meatballs.

SOUP:

2 (49-ounce) cans chicken broth
1 medium onion, chopped fine
¾ (1-pound) box acini de pepe
macaroni, cooked

1 (10-ounce) box frozen chopped
spinach, thawed
Salt and pepper to taste

Heat broth, onion, and macaroni in large saucepan. Drop in Meatballs, a few at a time, and cook ½ hour after all Meatballs are added. Add spinach; simmer 15 minutes. Add salt and pepper, if desired.

Judy Schnitzer (Great Southern Recipes)

Split Pea Soup

16 ounces split green peas
1 small end piece of ham or
ham bone
2 quarts water
Salt to taste

1 onion, halved
1 carrot, chunked
1 stalk celery, chunked
2 potatoes, peeled, cubed
Parsley sprigs to taste

Rinse peas well in cold water; drain. Combine peas, ham, water, salt, onion, carrot, celery, potatoes, and parsley in large saucepan. Bring to a boil; reduce heat. Simmer 1 hour, stirring occasionally. Remove onion, carrot, celery, and parsley before serving. May add additional water for desired consistency. Yields 6–8 servings.

Stella Malloy, Athens-Gainesville Council
(Lawfully Good Eating)

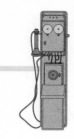

Italian Lentil Soup

1 (16-ounce) bag dry lentils
8 cups water
2 tablespoons olive oil
3 carrots, chopped
1 onion, chopped
1 clove garlic, minced
1 (28-ounce) can tomatoes,
 cut up, and liquid

1 teaspoon thyme
Salt and pepper to taste
2 celery stalks, cut up
½ (10-ounce) package frozen
 spinach, defrosted
⅓ pound crushed spaghetti,
 cooked
Parmesan or Romano cheese

Pick through beans; remove all foreign particles. Wash and drain.
Put in pot with water and simmer, covered. Heat olive oil in skillet; sauté carrots, onion, and garlic till onion is soft, but not brown.
Pour into pot with beans. Add tomatoes and liquid, thyme, salt,
pepper, and celery. Cover and simmer 1½ hours. Add spinach 5
minutes before finishing. Fold cooked spaghetti into finished
soup. Serve with Parmesan or Romano cheese.

Nancy Granieri (Great Southern Recipes)

Creamy Wild Rice Soup

⅓ cup wild rice
1 cup water
2½ teaspoons salt, divided
1 stick butter
¾ cup chopped onion

1 cup minced celery
¼ teaspoon white pepper
¼ cup all-purpose flour
5 cups milk
Chopped chives

Rinse wild rice. Bring water to a boil; add rice and ½ teaspoon salt. Reduce heat, cover, and simmer 30–45 minutes, or till tender. Melt butter in saucepan; add onion and celery. Cover and gently cook about 5 minutes, or till soft. Stir in remaining 2 teaspoons salt, pepper, and flour. Remove from heat and add milk, stirring till flour is well blended. Return to low heat. Cook, stirring till soup thickens. Add rice and simmer a few minutes more. Garnish with chives. Serves 6.

Ellen Brice, General (Dogwood Delights)

Cheese Soup

3 cups diced potatoes
1 cup water
½ cup sliced celery
½ cup sliced carrots
¼ cup diced onion
1 teaspoon parsley flakes

½ teaspoon salt
Dash of pepper
2 tablespoons all-purpose flour
1½ cups milk
½ pound Velveeta cheese,
    cubed

Cook all but flour, milk, and cheese till vegetables are tender. Gradually add flour to milk to make a paste; stir till smooth. Add to vegetables and cook till thick. Add Velveeta; stir till melted. Ready to serve. Good warmed over.

Joyce Stuart, Chamblee-North Fulton (Dogwood Delights II)

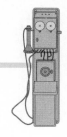

Cheesy Meatball Soup

MEATBALLS:

1 pound ground beef
¼ cup bread crumbs

1 egg
½ teaspoon Tabasco

Mix ingredients well; make into balls about the size of a quarter; set aside.

SOUP:

2 cups water
1 cup whole-kernel corn
1 cup chopped potato
1 cup chopped celery
½ cup sliced carrots

½ cup chopped onion
2 beef bouillon cubes
½ teaspoon Tabasco
1 (16-ounce) jar Cheez Whiz

Place Meatballs and all other ingredients, except Cheez Whiz, in slow cooker. Stir gently. Cover and cook on LOW 8–10 hours. Just before serving, add Cheez Whiz; stir gently till blended and serve.

Stella Colbert Hughes (Pat Hughes Thomas's mother),
Decatur-Tucker (Dogwood Delights II)

Broccoli Cheddar Soup

2 heads broccoli, chopped
4 cups chicken broth
2 cups heavy cream
2 bay leaves
1½ cups beer

1 cup grated sharp Cheddar
 cheese
Salt and Tabasco to taste
 (optional)

Cook broccoli in broth till tender; pour in blender or food processor. Scald cream with bay leaves. Add beer in steady stream. Add cheese, a little at a time. Add mixture to broccoli. Heat. DO NOT BOIL. Add salt and a touch of Tabasco, if desired.

Jean Hundley, Austell-Marietta (Dogwood Delights II)

Mom-Mom's
True Irish Potato Soup

1 pound hot pork sausage
1 large onion, chopped
3 stalks celery with leaves,
    chopped
2 cloves garlic, crushed
2 pounds potatoes, peeled, sliced

Salt and freshly ground pepper
    to taste
1 or 2 bay leaves
½ teaspoon celery seeds
1 cup milk

Brown sausage, onion, celery, and garlic. Drain; set aside. Cook potatoes in water (or chicken stock) to cover with salt and pepper till soft. Combine sausage mixture, potatoes and liquid. Add bay leaves and celery seeds. Cook slowly for 30 minutes. Add milk just before serving.

Brenda Plunkett, General (Dogwood Delights II)

Mushroom Soup

4 tablespoons butter
2 pounds fresh mushrooms,
    coarsely chopped
2 cloves garlic, minced
½ cup sliced green onions

Salt and pepper to taste
½ teaspon tarragon
5 cups chicken broth
½ cup dry Madeira wine
½ cup heavy cream

Heat butter in deep, heavy pot. Add mushrooms, garlic, and green onions, stirring to coat mushrooms with butter. Cook, stirring occasionally, for 15 minutes. Add salt, pepper, and tarragon. Add broth and bring to a boil Simmer for 30 minutes. Add Madeira wine; simmer 5 minutes more. Stir in cream. Taste and adjust seasonings. Serves 6–8.

Debbie Quakenbush, W.E.-BTL/Cable (Dogwood Delights)

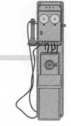

Onion Soup

3 tablespoons butter
1 tablespoon oil
6 cups sliced onions
1 teaspoon salt
½ teaspoon sugar
3 tablespoons flour

3 (10¾-ounce) cans beef broth
3 soup cans water
1 cup dry red or white wine
1 bay leaf
½ teaspoon sage
1 teaspoon pepper

Melt butter and oil in heavy 4-quart pan. Add onions and stir. Cover and cook over medium heat 15 minutes, stirring occasionally. When onions are tender and translucent, uncover, raise heat to medium-high, and stir in salt and sugar. Cook 20–30 minutes, stirring frequently, till onions are golden brown. Lower heat to medium. Stir in flour; cook and stir 2 minutes. Remove from heat. Heat broth and water; stir 1 cup into onion mixture. Add rest of broth, wine, bay leaf, sage, and pepper. Simmer slowly 5 minutes. Serve hot.

Amy Cromwell, General (Dogwood Delights)

French Onion Soup

6 large Vidalia onions, peeled,
  sliced thin
2 tablespoons butter, melted
3 (10-ounce) cans beef
  consommé

2 bouillon cubes
6 slices French bread, toasted
6 slices mozzarella cheese

Place onions in skillet with melted butter; sauté till glossy. Heat beef consommé; add bouillon cubes. Broil each side of French bread. Spoon onions into individual crocks till ⅔ full. Pour bouillon mixture over onions. Place 1 slice French bread toast on top of mixture. Place 1 slice cheese, folded, on top of toast. Broil in oven till melted; serve.

Sara Davis, General (Dogwood Delights II)

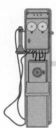

Chilled Berry Soup

1 quart fresh strawberries,
  hulled
⅓ cup ginger ale
¼ cup milk

⅓ cup sugar
1 tablespoon lemon juice
1 teaspoon vanilla
1 cup sour cream

Place strawberries in food processor or blender; cover and process till smooth. Add ginger ale, milk, sugar, lemon juice, and vanilla; cover and process till blended. Pour into bowl; whisk in sour cream till smooth. Cover and refrigerate till thoroughly chilled. Serves 4.

Bill Kent (Great Southern Recipes)

Spanish Gazpacho

3 medium green bell peppers,
  chopped
3 medium cucumbers, chopped
3 medium ripe tomatoes,
  chopped
2 medium red onions, chopped
2 cloves garlic, chopped
2 (10-ounce) cans tomato juice
  cocktail
3 teaspoons salt

½ teaspoon oregano
½ teaspoon basil
½ teaspoon Tabasco
1 tablespoon Worcestershire
½ cup oil
½ cup red wine vinegar
2 tablespoons lemon juice
Sour cream for garnish
  (optional)

Mix all ingredients; refrigerate 2 hours. Take 2 cups of the mixture and put in blender; purée about 15 seconds. Stir purée and remaining mixture together. Chill. Garnish with sour cream and croutons, if desired.

Marilyn Jeffries, General (Dogwood Delights)

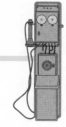

Fish Chowder

2½ pounds fish (fresh or
frozen catfish, flounder,
bass, etc.)
2 Irish potatoes, peeled, diced
1 large onion, diced
3 teaspoons salt
1½ teaspoons finely ground
pepper

3 heaping tablespoons ketchup
2½ tablespoons
Worcestershire
¾ stick margarine
5 dashes hot sauce
3½ cups milk

Place fish in 8- to 10-quart pot; just cover with water. Boil slowly till fish is done. Keep foam skimmed. Remove fish and save stock. Tear fish into small pieces and remove all bones. Replace to stock. Add all remaining ingredients except milk. Add more water, if needed, to boil ingredients. Keep covered and boil slowly about 1½ hours. Turn heat on low and add milk. Cook on low heat about 20 minutes.

Clyde Roundtree, W.E.-Region (Dogwood Delights)

Shrimp Chowder

4 cups water
1 medium onion, chopped
1 small leek, chopped
2 stalks celery, diced
1 carrot, diced
1 medium potato, peeled, diced

8 ounces salmon, diced
1 pound baby shrimp, peeled
¼ teaspoon cayenne
Salt and pepper to taste
¼ cup heavy cream
2 tablespoons sherry (optional)

In large saucepan, bring water to a boil; add vegetables. Cook 10 minutes. Add salmon; simmer 5 minutes. Fold in shrimp and seasonings. Continue cooking 2 minutes. Stir in cream, mixing till well blended. Add sherry, if desired. Reheat without boiling. Serve. Yields 6 servings.

Cathy Wanat (Great Southern Recipes)

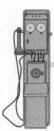

Sausage-Bean Chowder

2 pounds bulk pork sausage
4 cups water
2 (16-ounce) cans pinto beans
2 (14½-ounce) cans whole
  tomatoes, undrained,
  chopped
2 medium onions, chopped
2 medium potatoes, peeled,
  cubed

½ cup chopped bell pepper
  (green or red)
1 large bay leaf
½ teaspoon salt
½ teaspoon dried whole thyme
¼ teaspoon garlic powder
¼ teaspoon pepper

Brown sausage in Dutch oven, stirring to crumble; drain. Stir in remaining ingredients; bring to a boil. Cover, reduce heat, and simmer 1 hour. Remove bay leaf before serving. Yields 3 quarts.

Jan Wittcheck, Area (Dogwood Delights II)

Ham Chowder

2 cups diced ham
1 onion, chopped
1 (15-ounce) can cream-style
  corn
3 cups water

2 cups diced potatoes
1 cup tomato juice
1 (8-ounce) can tomato sauce
1 cup milk
Salt and pepper to taste

Fry ham and onion in saucepan till onion is browned. Add corn, water, and potatoes; bring to a boil. Simmer till potatoes are done. Add tomato juice, tomato sauce, milk, and salt and pepper. Add more water, if needed, as some potatoes require more water. If thickening is needed, add a paste of 2 tablespoons flour and water.

Barbara Keel, Conyers, GA (Great Southern Recipes)

Chicken Corn Chowder

1 cup chicken stock
1 cup heavy cream
1 cup milk
2 chicken breasts, cooked, diced
1 pound russet potatoes, cooked, diced

2 cups frozen corn kernels
⅛ cup diced onion
⅛ cup diced red bell pepper
1 chicken bouillon cube
2 teaspoons sugar
⅛ cup chopped fresh parsley
2 teaspoons hot sauce

Bring chicken stock to a boil; add cream, milk, chicken, potatoes, corn, onion, pepper, bouillon cube, and sugar; simmer 40 minutes. Add parsley and hot sauce and simmer 5 minutes more. Serve hot. Serves 8.

Bill Kent (Great Southern Recipes)

Lobster Bisque

1 (10¾-ounce) can cream of asparagus soup
1 (10¾-ounce) can cream of mushroom soup

1½ soup cans light cream
1 (8-ounce) can lobster meat
3–4 tablespoons sherry
Sliced lemon

Combine first 4 ingredients in double boiler; mix well. Heat over simmering water, stirring frequently. Stir in sherry. Ladle into soup bowls. Garnish with lemon slices. Yields 4–6 servings.

Judy Moody, Augusta Council (Lawfully Good Eating)

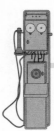

Seafood Gumbo

½ teaspoon each: cayenne
  pepper, ground white pepper,
  ground black pepper
1½ teaspoons paprika
½ teaspoon dried thyme
½ teaspoon dried oregano
1 bay leaf, crushed
1 teaspoon salt
¾ cup oil
2 cups chopped onions
2 cups chopped green bell
  peppers

2 cups chopped celery
1 teaspoon minced garlic
3 tablespoons filé powder
2 teaspoons hot pepper sauce
1½ cups tomato sauce
7 cups seafood gumbo stock
2 cups shucked oysters
1 cup crabmeat
1 pound small shrimp, peeled,
  deveined

Combine red, white, and black peppers, paprika, thyme, oregano, bay leaf, and salt; set aside.

In a 5-quart or larger pot, heat oil over medium heat, warming pot first. Add onions, green peppers, and celery. Turn to high heat. Stirring frequently, add garlic, filé, hot sauce, and pepper-herb mixture. Cook 5 minutes, stirring constantly. Add tomato sauce and stir as it reduces over high heat. Add seafood gumbo stock and bring to a boil.

Reduce heat and simmer 1 hour, stirring occasionally. When ready to serve, add oysters, crabmeat, and shrimp. Cover and wait 5 minutes. Turn off heat and let stand 10 minutes. Serve.

Laverne Motes (Great Southern Recipes)

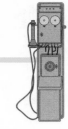

Oven Beef Stew

2 pounds lean beef, cut into
bite-size pieces
¼ teaspoon pepper
¼ teaspoon garlic powder
½ teaspoon basil
1 tablespoon parsley flakes
2 medium onions, cut into
chunks
3 or 4 stalks celery, cut in 1-inch
pieces

6 carrots, cut in 1-inch pieces
4 or 5 potatoes, cut into bite-size
pieces
1 tablespoon sugar (optional)
3 tablespoons tapioca
1 (12-ounce) can V-8, or 1
(18-ounce) can tomato juice

Place meat in a 3-quart casserole; sprinkle with pepper, garlic, basil, and parsley. Add onions on top of meat, then celery, carrots, and potatoes. Sprinkle with sugar and tapioca. Pour juice over all. Cover tightly and bake 3 hours at 325°. Serves 6–8.

Debbie Giddens (Network), Atlanta-Buckhead
(Dogwood Delights II)

Brunswick Stew

1½ pounds lean ground beef
½ pound lean ground pork or
sausage
3 or 4 large onions, chopped
1 pound cooked chicken,
chopped
2 cups chicken broth
2 pounds potatoes, peeled,
chopped

3 (20-ounce) cans tomatoes
1 (20-ounce) can corn
½ (8-ounce) can sliced okra
Tabasco to taste
Salt and pepper to taste
2 tablespoons chili powder
⅛ cup vinegar
1 (20-ounce) can lima beans

Brown beef and pork with onions; drain. Add remaining ingredients and cook 3–4 hours over slow simmer till stew achieves a thick, smooth texture. Stir often.

Don Eargle, General (Dogwood Delights)

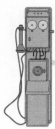

Mulligan's Stew

1 pound ground beef
1 pound hot pork sausage
2 (16-ounce) cans pork and
  beans
2 (14½-ounce) cans tomatoes

1 (15-ounce) can whole-kernel
  corn
1 (15-ounce) can cream-style
  corn

Brown beef and sausage in saucepan; drain. Add remaining ingredients and simmer 1 hour.

Edna Whaley, Austell-Marietta (Dogwood Delights)

Newfee Oyster Stew American-Style

10 slices bacon
1 large onion, chopped
3 tablespoons all-purpose flour
1 (12-ounce) can beer
3 cups milk
2 (12-ounce) cans evaporated
  milk

3 (8-ounce) cans salt-and-
  water-packed whole oysters,
  chopped
1 tablespoon pepper
1 teaspoon salt

Fry bacon in large saucepan till crispy. Drain on paper towels, reserving 3–4 tablespoons pan drippings. Sauté onion in pan drippings till tender. Stir in flour. Cook till golden, stirring constantly. Stir in beer and milk. Cook till bubbly, but do not boil, stirring constantly. Remove from heat. Add oysters, pepper, and salt; mix well. Cook till heated through. Ladle into soup tureen; sprinkle with crumbled bacon. Yield 8–10 servings.

Dianne Fitzgerald, Augusta Council (Lawfully Good Eating)

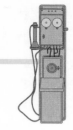

Chili

1 pound ground beef	1 (64-ounce) can V-8 juice
1 medium onion, chopped	2 (16-ounce) cans chili beans
1 green bell pepper, chopped	6 tablespoons chili powder

Brown beef, onions, and peppers in skillet. Transfer to crockpot. Add V-8 juice, beans, and chili powder. Cook approximately 4 hours on HIGH.

Raymond McNure, Jonesboro-South Fulton
(Dogwood Delights II)

Jack's Coathanger Chili

2 pounds hamburger meat	1 (1¼-ounce) package chili mix
1 (28-ounce) can whole tomatoes, chopped up in pot	1 (16-ounce) can pinto beans
	2 large onions, wedged
1 (10-ounce) can tomatoes and green chiles	Garlic salt to taste (optional)
1 (1¼-ounce) package taco seasoning mix	

Cook hamburger meat; drain. Place meat in large stockpot; add remaining ingredients. Cook over slow heat a minimum of 2 hours. For better flavor, after cooking and cool down, refrigerate 24 hours before slowly heating and serving.

Note: Great to fill tacos, enchiladas or burritos.

Jack Thompson, W.E.-BTL/Cable (Dogwood Delights)

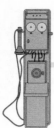

Hot Shot Turkey Chili

2 pounds ground turkey
1 large onion, chopped
1 tablespoon olive oil
2 clove garlic, minced
1/4 cup sugar
2 bay leaves
2 cups water
¼ teaspoon cayenne pepper

2 tablespoons chili powder
1 (28-ounce) can tomatoes
1 (16-ounce) can tomatoes
3 (16-ounce) cans pinto beans
1 (8-ounce) can tomatoes and
   green chilies
2 (4-ounce) cans chopped
   green chilies

Brown turkey and onion in olive oil in 5-quart saucepan, stirring frequently. Add remaining ingredients. Simmer for 45 minutes, stirring occasionally. Remove bay leaves. Serves 10–12.

Gene Hodge, Sheriff of Muscogee County (Lawfully Good Eating)

$\mathcal{S}$alads

1892
Desk Set

The first common battery arrange-
ment came into play in the 1890s,
providing electricity to all telephones
controlled by the central office. Previously,
each customer's telephone needed its own battery to
power the transmitter. The innovation of the common battery changed telephone design. The big, bulky wall sets
with wet batteries providing power and cranks to signal
the operator could now be replaced with sleek desk sets.
Since the crank and batteries were no longer required, the
subset could be mounted on the wall and out of the way.
When you wanted to place a call, you would simply pick
up the receiver and wait for the operator. When you finished your call, you could just hang up. Long-distance calling reached a major milestone in 1892, when telephone
service between New York and Chicago began.   This
950–mile circuit was the longest line possible with the exist-
ing technology.

Chicken Salad with Grapes

10-ounces boned, cooked
  chicken
2 stalks celery, chopped
1 small onion, chopped fine
½ cup split seedless white
  grapes

½ cup mayonnaise
Salt and pepper to taste
¼ cup toasted almonds

Mix all ingredients except grapes and almonds. Fold in grapes.
Serve on lettuce leaves. Garnish with toasted almonds. Serves 4.

Marilyn Jeffries, General (Dogwood Delights)

Almond Chicken Salad

4 cups cubed cooked chicken
1 cup chopped celery
2 hard-boiled eggs, chopped
½ cup mayonnaise
¼ cup sour cream
1 teaspoon salt

½ teaspoon pepper
⅓ teaspoon celery salt
⅛ teaspoon dry mustard
⅛ teaspoon paprika
½ cup slivered almonds,
  toasted

Combine chicken, celery, and eggs. Combine remainder of ingredients, except almonds; stir till smooth. Pour over chicken mixture and toss gently. Stir in almonds and serve immediately, or refrigerate and add almonds right before serving.

Sherry Scott, Marietta, GA (Great Southern Recipes)

Tropical Chicken Salad

2 cups cubed cooked chicken
1 cup chopped celery
1 cup mayonnaise
½–1 teaspoon curry powder
1 (20-ounce) can chunk
   pineapple, drained

2 large firm bananas, sliced
1 (11-ounce) can Mandarin
   oranges, drained
½ cup flaked coconut
¾ cup salted cashews

Place chicken and celery in large bowl. Combine mayonnaise and curry powder; add to chicken mixture; mix well. Cover and chill at least 30 minutes.

Just before serving, add pineapple, bananas, oranges, and coconut. Toss gently. Serve on salad greens, if desired. Sprinkle with nuts. Yields 4–6 servings.

Brenda Borland, Social Circle, GA (Great Southern Recipes)

Mexican Cornbread Salad

It tastes like cornbread dressing, except the veggies are not cooked.

2 (6-ounce) packages Mexican
   cornbread mix
1 (15-ounce) can whole-kernel
   corn, undrained
1 onion, chopped
1 green bell pepper, chopped
1½ cups fresh tomatoes,
   chopped
¼ teaspoon celery seed or
   leaves

1 cup grated Cheddar cheese
4 or 5 slices bacon, cooked,
   crumbled
3 hard-boiled eggs, chopped
1 teaspoon Italian seasoning
Salt and pepper to taste
1 teaspoon parsley flakes
   (optional)
1 cup mayonnaise or buttermilk
   salad dressing

Make cornbread by package directions; cool; crumble into bowl. Mix other ingredients; chill overnight. Serve cold. Makes 10–12 servings.

Arlene Davis, Decatur-Tucker (Dogwood Delights II)

Chili Cornbread Salad

1 (8½-ounce) package
  cornbread muffin mix
1 (4-ounce) can chopped green
  chiles, undrained
⅛ teaspoon ground cumin
⅛ teaspoon dried oregano
Pinch of rubbed sage
1 cup mayonnaise
1 cup sour cream
1 envelope ranch salad dressing
  mix

2 (15-ounce) cans Mexicorn,
  drained
2 (15-ounce) cans pinto beans,
  drained, rinsed
3 medium tomatoes, chopped
1 cup chopped green bell pepper
1 cup chopped green onions
10 bacon strips, cooked,
  crumbled (or bacon bits)
2 cups shredded Cheddar cheese

Prepare cornbread batter according to package directions. Stir in chiles, cumin, oregano, and sage. Pour into a greased 8-inch square baking pan (or muffin pan). Bake at 400° for 20–25 minutes or till done. Cool.

Combine mayonnaise, sour cream, and dressing mix; set aside. Crumble half the cornbread into a 9x13-inch dish. Layer with half the corn, mayonnaise mixture, beans, tomatoes, green pepper, onions, bacon, and cheese. Repeat layers. Cover and refrigerate at least 2 hours. Serves 10–12.

Note: May like to double mayonnaise, sour cream, and dressing mix.

Brenda Harris, Loganville, GA (Great Southern Recipes)

Vegetable Salad

1 (15-ounce) can cut green
beans
1 (8-ounce) can LeSueur green
peas
1 medium green bell pepper,
chopped

1 medium onion, chopped fine
1 cup chopped celery
1 (2-ounce) jar chopped
pimentos
Salt to taste

Drain vegetables well; mix in bowl and sprinkle with salt. Let sit in refrigerator overnight, covered. Drain again next day.

DRESSING:

1 cup sugar
1 cup vinegar

½ cup oil

Combine ingredients and marinate vegetables. Will keep 2 weeks in refrigerator.

Doris Thompson, Grayson, GA (Great Southern Recipes)

In 1877, Bell Telephone Company was formed to operate local telephone exchange operation, installing the first city exchange in Hartford, Connecticut.

New Potato Salad

1 pound new potatoes
¼ cup (heaping) mayonnaise
1 tablespoon finely chopped
  celery
1 tablespoon chopped pickle or
  pickle relish

1–2 tablespoons natural yogurt
  or sunflower oil
Salt and pepper to taste
2 tablespoons chopped parsley

Scrub potatoes, but do not peel. Boil potatoes in water to cover in saucepan 15 minutes, or till tender; drain. Cool to room temperature. Cut into quarters; place in large salad bowl. Combine mayonnaise, celery, pickle, yogurt, salt and pepper; mix well. Add to potatoes, tossing gently to coat potatoes. Garnish with parsley. Serve immediately, or chill before serving. Yields 8 servings.

Jackie Joyner, Athens-Gainesville Council
(Lawfully Good Eating)

Creamy Potato Salad

⅓ cup clear Italian dressing
7 medium potatoes, cooked in
  jackets, peeled, diced
¾ cup sliced celery
⅓ cup sliced green onions
  and tops
4 hard-boiled eggs
½ cup mayonnaise
1 cup sour cream

1½ teaspoons prepared
  horseradish mustard
2–3 strips crisp-fried bacon,
  crumbled (optional)
1–2 chopped dill pickles
  (optional)
Salt and pepper to taste
Celery seeds to taste
Paprika

Pour dressing over warm potatoes; chill 2 hours. Add celery and onions. Chop egg whites; add. Sieve yolks; mix with mayonnaise, sour cream, and horseradish mustard. Fold into salad. Add salt, pepper, and celery seeds to taste. Sprinkle paprika on top. Cover and chill at least 2 hours. Better if overnight.

Tony Kubiak, General (Dogwood Delights II)

Three Bean Salad

1 (15-ounce) can red kidney
  beans, drained
1 (15-ounce) can white wax
  beans, drained
1 (15-ounce) can cut green
  beans, drained
1 large white onion, sliced thin

1 cup apple cider vinegar
¾ cup water
1 cup sugar
¼ cup oil
2 teaspoons whole cloves
½ teaspoon salt
¼ teaspoon black pepper

Place all vegetables in bowl. Combine remaining ingredients in saucepan and bring to a boil. Cool. Pour over bean mixture. Refrigerate at least 12 hours before serving. Serves 6.

Ruth E. Fowler, General (Dogwood Delights)

Seven Layer Salad

6 cups shredded lettuce
1 (4-ounce) can sliced
  mushrooms, drained
1 cup coarsely chopped celery
1 cup coarsely chopped green
  bell pepper
1 large red onion, sliced into
  rings

1 (8-ounce) can English peas,
  drained
1 cup mayonnaise
2½ cups grated Cheddar
  cheese
Bacon bits

Prepare vegetables and layer ingredients in a large bowl, starting with lettuce and ending with bacon bits. Chill till serving time.

Donna Thomson, Brookwood-Downtown (Dogwood Delights)

Overnight Salad

1 head cauliflower, chopped
1 head lettuce, chopped
1 medium onion, chopped
1 cup mayonnaise

½ cup grated Parmesan cheese
1 pound bacon, crisp-fried,
  crumbled

Combine cauliflower, lettuce, and onion; mix well. Spread mayonnaise over top; sprinkle with cheese and bacon. Chill, tightly covered, overnight. Yields 12 servings.

Jeri Lavender, Macon Council (Lawfully Good Eating)

Broccoli Salad

½ cup mayonnaise
2 tablespoons vinegar
¼ cup sugar
1 bunch broccoli, chopped
3 tablespoons imitation bacon
  bits, or 10 slices bacon, fried
  crisp, crumbled

2–5 green onions, chopped
½ cup grated Cheddar cheese
  (optional)
½ cup chopped nuts (optional)
½ cup raisins
Dash of salt

Make dressing with mayonnaise, vinegar, and sugar. Mix all other ingredients, and toss with dressing. Chill and serve.

Helen Russell, General (Dogwood Delights II)

Spring Strawberry Spinach Salad

1 bag baby spinach
10 large strawberries, sliced
1 tablespoon poppy seeds
½ cup Splenda or sugar

1 teaspoon salt
⅓ cup white wine vinegar
1 cup oil

Mix spinach and strawberries. Stir in poppy seeds. In blender, combine remaining ingredients. Pour over salad right before serving.

Pam Williams, Covington, GA (Great Southern Recipes)

Cranberry Spinach Salad

1 tablespoon butter
¾ cup blanched, slivered
   almonds
2 tablespoons toasted sesame
   seeds
1 tablespoon poppy seeds
½ cup sugar or Splenda

2 teaspoons minced onion
¼ teaspoon paprika
¼ cup white wine vinegar
¼ cup cider vinegar
½ cup oil
1 bag baby spinach
1 cup dried cranberries

In medium saucepan, melt butter over medium heat; cook and stir almonds till lightly toasted.

Whisk together sesame seeds, poppy seeds, sugar, onion, paprika, white wine vinegar, cider vinegar, and oil. Toss with spinach, cranberries, and almonds just before serving.

Pam Williams, Covington, GA (Great Southern Recipes)

Blueberry Congealed Salad

1 (6-ounce) package cherry
Jell-O
2 cups boiling water
1 (15-ounce) can blueberries,
drained, reserve liquid
1 (8-ounce) can crushed
pineapple, drained, reserve
liquid

1 (8-ounce) package cream
cheese, softened
½ cup powdered sugar
½ pint sour cream
½ teaspoon vanilla
½ cup chopped nuts

Dissolve Jell-O in boiling water. Add enough water to reserved fruit juices to make 1 cup liquid. Add Jell-O mix; stir in blueberries and pineapple. Pour into 2-quart flat pan. Cover and refrigerate to set.

Combine cream cheese, sugar, sour cream, and vanilla. Spread over salad. Sprinkle with nuts.

Helen Atherton, Area-Perimeter (Dogwood Delights II); Lillian Wilbands, Chamblee-North Fulton (Dogwood Delights)

Cherry Cola Salad

½ cup water
1 (21-ounce) can cherry pie
  filling
1 (6-ounce) package cherry
  Jell-O

1 (15-ounce) can crushed
  pineapple
1 cup chopped pecans
1 (6-ounce) bottle cola

Add water to pie filling and boil 5 minutes. Add undiluted Jell-O while pie filling is still hot. Set aside to cool. When cool, add pineapple, pecans, and cola. Pour into 9x13-inch dish and chill well.

Jamie Langston, Chamblee-North Fulton (Dogwood Delights)

Cranberry Salad

1 cup sugar
1 cup ground raw cranberries
1 (3-ounce) package lemon
  Jell-O
½ cup boiling water
1 cup orange juice

2 teaspoons grated orange rind
1 (8-ounce) can crushed
  pineapple, drained
½ cup broken pecans
1 cup chopped celery

Mix sugar and cranberries together and let stand several hours. Add Jell-O to boiling water and stir till dissolved. Add orange juice and stir, then add cranberries and remaining ingredients; pour into mold. Chill.

Dorothy L. Witt, General (Dogwood Delights)

Strawberry Congealed Salad

2 (10-ounce) packages frozen
  strawberries, divided
2 (3-ounce) packages strawberry
  Jell-O, divided
2 (8-ounce) cans crushed
  pineapple, divided

½ cup boiling water
2 (8-ounce) cartons sour cream,
  divided

Mix 1 package strawberries, 1 package Jell-O, 1 can crushed pineapple, and ½ cup boiling water. Let congeal. Cover mixture with 1 container of sour cream. Repeat mixing of strawberries, Jell-O, and pineapple. Let congeal. Layer with last carton of sour cream.

Cherry Strickland, Austell-Marietta (Dogwood Delights II)

Sweetheart Salad

1 envelope unflavored gelatin
1 (20-ounce) can crushed
  pineapple, undrained
1 (8-ounce) can crushed
  pineapple, undrained
½ cup sugar

2 (3-ounce) packages cream
  cheese, softened
1 (4-ounce) jar maraschino
  cherries, chopped
1 cup whipping cream
Sugar to taste

Soften gelatin in undrained pineapple in saucepan. Add sugar. Bring to a boil, stirring frequently. Stir in cream cheese and maraschino cherries. Cool to room temperature. Spoon into bowl. Chill till partially set. Beat whipping cream in mixer bowl till soft peaks form, adding additional sugar to taste, if desired. Fold into gelatin mixture. Spoon into serving bowl. Chill till serving time. Yields 6 servings.

Louise Scott, Columbus Life Member Club
(Lawfully Good Eating)

Heavenly Orange Salad

2 (3-ounce) packages orange
   Jell-O
2½ cups boiling water
40 small marshmallows
½ cup sugar
2 (8-ounce) cans crushed
   pineapple, undrained

1 (16-ounce) carton Cool Whip
1 teaspoon vanilla
1 tablespoon mayonnaise
½ cup chopped nuts
1 cup grated cheese

Heat together first 4 ingredients. Add crushed pineapple with juice. Cool till partially set. Add remaining ingredients and put in large mold to congeal. Serves 12.

Loretta Mosteller, Brookwood-Downtown (Dogwood Delights)

Twenty-Four Hour Salad

2 eggs, beaten
4 tablespoons vinegar
2 tablespoons butter
1 cup whipped cream or Cool
   Whip

2 cups halved white cherries
2 cups pineapple chunks
2 oranges, cut in pieces
2 cups small marshmallows

Put eggs in double boiler; add vinegar and beat constantly till thick and smooth. Remove from heat; add butter and allow to cool. When cool, fold in whipped cream or Cool Whip and fruit mixture. Put in refrigerator for 24 hours before serving. Serves 10.

Mary Jo Rainey, General (Dogwood Delights)

Ambrosia

Everyone will think you peeled oranges for days for this recipe.

3 yellow Delicious apples,
  peeled, grated
1 (6-ounce) can concentrated
  orange juice

2½ cans water
6 ounces flaked coconut
1 (8-ounce) can crushed
  pineapple, undrained

Mix all ingredients together. Place in refrigerator and serve cold.

Reba S. Howard, Area (Dogwood Delights II)

Orange Fluff Stuff Salad

1 (8-ounce) whipped topping
1 (3-ounce) package orange
  gelatin
1 (16-ounce) carton cottage
  cheese

1 (16-ounce) can juice-pack
  crushed pineapple, drained
1 (11-ounce) can Mandarin
  oranges, drained

Combine whipped topping and gelatin; mix well. Add cottage cheese and pineapple; mix well. Pour into serving dish. Top with Mandarin oranges. Chill in refrigerator till serving time. Yields 6 servings.

Linda M. Grown, Macon Council (Lawfully Good Eating)

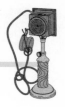

Watergate Salad

1 (12-ounce) container Cool
  Whip
1 cup miniature marshmallows
1 (20-ounce) can crushed
  pineapple, undrained

1 (3-ounce) package pistachio
  instant pudding mix
1 cup broken pecans

Mix all ingredients together and refrigerate.

Janice Davis, Austell-Marietta (Dogwood Delights II)

Applesauce Salad

1 (6-ounce) package raspberry
  or strawberry gelatin
1 (16-ounce) can applesauce
1 (10-ounce) can diet cola
1 (8-ounce) can crushed
  pineapple, undrained

1 cup chopped pecans
1 cup chopped cherries
Miniature marshmallows

Combine gelatin and applesauce in saucepan. Heat till gelatin is dissolved, stirring constantly. Cool 25–30 minutes. Add cola, pineapple, pecans, and cherries, stirring to mix. Pour into serving bowl; cover top with miniature marshmallows. Chill in refrigerator 2 hours or till congealed. Yields 6–8 servings.

Ruth Bracewell, Macon Council (Lawfully Good Eating)

Thanksgiving Salad

2 (3-ounce) packages lemon
  gelatin
2 cups boiling water
1 (8-ounce) package cream
  cheese, softened

1 cup sour cream
1 (20-ounce) can crushed
  pineapple
1 cup finely chopped celery
½ cup chopped nuts

Dissolve gelatin in boiling water in mixer bowl. Chill till partially set. Beat gelatin till light and fluffy. Add cream cheese and sour cream; beat well. Stir in pineapple, celery, and nuts. Chill, covered, in refrigerator till set. May keep in refrigerator for several days. Yields 10 servings.

Betty Brown, Athens-Gainesville Council
(Lawfully Good Eating)

Green Apple Salad

1 (20-ounce) can crushed
  pineapple with juice
¾ cup sugar
½ cup self-rising flour
2 tablespoons margarine

2 Granny Smith apples, diced
1 (8-ounce) package cream
  cheese, softened
1 (12-ounce) carton Cool Whip
Chopped walnuts

Mix pineapple and juice, sugar, flour, and margarine in saucepan; cook on medium till thickened, stirring often. Add apples and pour mixture into serving dish. Top with cream cheese mixed with Cool Whip. Sprinkle with chopped walnuts. Refrigerate. Serves 6.

Martha Jung LM, Buford, GA (Great Southern Recipes)

Phyllis' Fruit Salad

2 tablespoons mayonnaise
1 (8-ounce) tub whipped cream
  cheese
1 (8-ounce) carton Cool Whip,
  partially thawed

1 (11-ounce) can Mandarin
  oranges, drained
1 (20-ounce) can crushed
  pineapple, drained
1 cup miniature marshmallows

Cream mayonnaise and cream cheese; add Cool Whip and blend. Add oranges, pineapple, and marshmallows. Chill. Best if eaten within 24 hours.

Phillis Yancey, Decatur, GA (Great Southern Recipes)

Frozen Cranberry Salad

2 cups cranberries
1 orange, peeled
1 cup sugar
1 (8-ounce) can crushed
  pineapple, drained
1 (8-ounce) package cream
  cheese, softened

½ cup mayonnaise
¼ teaspoon salt
½ cup chopped pecans
1 cup whipped cream
2 cups mini marshmallows

Grind cranberries and orange; add sugar and mix well. Add remaining ingredients; mix well. Pour into a 8x8-inch dish and freeze. Cut into squares; serve frozen.

Brownie Scott, Marietta, GA (Great Southern Recipes)

Frozen Fruit Salad

1 (16-ounce) carton sour cream
2 tablespoons lemon juice
¾ cup sugar
⅛ teaspoon salt
3 bananas, peeled, cubed

1 (8-ounce) can crushed
  pineapple, undrained
¼ cup chopped cherries
¼ cup chopped pecans

Combine all ingredients and pour into muffin tins lined with paper liners. Freeze till firm. Store in plastic bag. Makes about 1½ dozen.

Pam Burnett, Brookwood-Downtown (Dogwood Delights)

Frozen Salad

1 (8-ounce) can crushed
  pineapple
1 (14-ounce) can sweetened
  condensed milk
1 cup chopped nuts

2 (10-ounce) packages frozen
  strawberries, thawed
2 bananas, sliced
1 (8-ounce) carton whipped
  topping

Combine first 5 ingredients in bowl; mix well. Fold in whipped topping. Spray Bundt pan with nonstick cooking spray. Spoon mixture into pan. Freeze, covered, till firm. Unmold onto serving plate. Yields 8 servings.

Joyce Kerce, Rome Council (Lawfully Good Eating)

Cole Slaw

1 head green cabbage, thinly
  sliced
1 tomato, diced
1 cucumber, diced
2 carrots, thinly sliced

2 teaspoons celery seeds
1 teaspoon lemon pepper
1 (8-ounce) bottle Viva Italian
  salad dressing

Toss all ingredients except dressing. Shake salad dressing over slaw and toss well. Chill.

Janice Grant, Austell-Marietta (Dogwood Delights II)

Chinese Coleslaw

1 package pre-cut cabbage slaw
  mix
2 packages chicken ramen
  noodles

1 package sunflower seeds
1 package sliced almonds

DRESSING:
½ cup apple cider vinegar
½ cup sugar

Packet from ramen noodles

Mix together cabbage, ramen noodles, sunflower seeds, and almonds. When ready to serve, mix Dressing ingredients and add to dry mixture.

Peggy Hovorka, Lithonia, GA (Great Southern Recipes)

Grace's Hot Salsa

1 gallon tomatoes (fresh or
   stewed)
6 large onions, diced
5 or 6 bell peppers, diced

12 hot peppers, diced
2½ cups vinegar
2¼ cups sugar

Combine all ingredients and cook on medium heat for 2½ hours, stirring often to keep from sticking. Cook longer if you want it to be thicker. Put in canning jars while hot, using sealing lids.

Grace Chester, Decatur-Tucker (Dogwood Delights II)

Pickled Vidalia Onion Relish

4 quarts finely chopped Vidalia
   onions
1 large head cabbage, chopped
   fine
4 medium green peppers,
   chopped

1 cup pickling salt
1 gallon water
5 cups sugar
2 teaspoons turmeric
6 tablespoons dry mustard
1 quart vinegar

Mix first 5 ingredients in order listed. Soak mixture in refrigerator overnight. Next day, bring mixture to a boil; drain well. To drained mixture, add remaining ingredients and cook about 15 minutes (boiling). Pack hot relish in hot jars and seal

Louise Bonner, W. E.-Service/Installation (Dogwood Delights)

Green Tomato Pickles

7 pounds green tomatoes
1 cup slaked lime (pickling
    lime)
10 cups sugar

1 quart vinegar
½ package cinnamon sticks
1 teaspoon mace
1 teaspoon whole cloves

Wash and slice tomatoes ⅛ inch thick. Combine with lime and cold water to cover in large container. Let stand 24 hours. Rinse; cover with cold water. Soak 6 hours longer; drain. Repeat. Combine sugar, vinegar, cinnamon sticks, mace, and cloves in large bowl; mix well. Pour over tomatoes; let stand 12 hours. Bring to a boil in saucepan over medium heat. Boil 20 minutes, stirring frequently. Spoon into hot sterilized jars, leaving ½-inch headspace; seal with 2-piece lids. Yields 10 pints.

Maggie Cameron, Macon Council (Lawfully Good Eating)

Bread and Butter Pickles

1 gallon sliced cucumbers
1 quart sliced onions
Water
2 cups lime
5 cups vinegar

5 cups sugar
1 cup water
½ cup salt
⅔ box pickling spices
Mustard seeds

Soak cucumbers and onions for 24 hours in water and 2 cups lime. Pour off and rinse 3 or 4 times with cold water. Soak for 3 hours in cold water. Pour water off.

Bring vinegar, sugar, 1 cup water, and salt to a boil. Add pickling spices, onions and cucumbers. Simmer while stirring, 10–15 minutes till color starts to change. Add 1 teaspoon mustard seeds per quart. Pack pickles in hot jars. Pour liquid till ¼ inch from top and seal.

Sandy Saxton, General (Dogwood Delights II)

Sweet Potato Salad

8 small sweet potatoes
½–¾ teaspoon salt
2 (8-ounce) cans sliced
　pineapple
½ cup golden raisins

2 egg yolks
½–¾ cup packed brown
　sugar
¼ cup apple cider vinegar
¾ cup oil

Combine sweet potatoes and water to cover by 1 inch in large saucepan. Add salt. Bring to a boil; reduce heat; simmer 15 minutes, or till tip of knife slices easily into potatoes, stirring occasionally. Drain; place under cold running water briefly to stop cooking. Cool completely. Peel sweet potatoes; cut into ⅜-inch slices. Place in shallow serving dish. Drain pineapple, reserving ½ cup juice. Cut pineapple into wedges. Sprinkle pineapple and raisins over sweet potatoes.

Combine egg yolks, brown sugar, reserved ½ cup pineapple juice, and vinegar in blender container. Process while adding oil in slow steady stream. Pour dressing over potatoes. Chill, covered, for several hours, stirring gently several times to coat all ingredients. (To avoid using raw eggs, use the equivalent amount of egg substitute.) Yields 12–16 servings.

Brenda Burton, Athens-Gainesville Council
(Lawfully Good Eating)

$\mathcal{V}$egetables

1919
Candlestick

The first dial telephone exchange is credited to Almon B. Strowger who introduced it in LaPorte, Indiana, in 1892. However, it was many years before switching equipment was sufficiently developed to permit dial installation in larger cities. The advent of the vacuum tube amplifier (or repeater) made lines of any length feasible. With repeaters in the line, transcontinental telephone service opened in 1915. Dial service was coming in strongly, and customers could now dial out themselves, with no need to go through an operator. The first dial phones were candlestick phones. To place a call, you lifted the receiver, waited for dial tone, then dialed. The dial tone was a much lower pitched tone than what we hear today. If the switching equipment was busy, dial tone might take several seconds to come on.

Broccoli and Rice Casserole

1 (10-ounce) box frozen,
  chopped broccoli
1 cup chopped onion
1 cup chopped celery
3 tablespoons butter
1 (10¾-ounce) can cream of
  chicken soup

1 soup can milk
1 (4-ounce) jar cheese spread
1 package yellow rice mix, or 2
  cups cooked white rice

Thaw broccoli in hot water; drain well. Sauté onion and celery in butter. Add soup, milk, and cheese spread; simmer till hot. Add to rice and drained broccoli; mix well. Put in lightly greased casserole dish. Bake 30–40 minutes in 350° oven. Serves 10–12.

Note: Can be made ahead and refrigerated or frozen. If frozen, thaw before baking.

Liz Stephan, W. E. BTL/Cable (Dogwood Delights)

Broccoli Soufflé

2 (10-ounce) packages frozen
  chopped broccoli
1 (10¾-ounce) can cream of
  mushroom soup
6 eggs, beaten

1 cup mayonnaise
1 tablespoon minced onion
Salt and pepper to taste
½ cup shredded sharp Cheddar
  cheese

Cook broccoli using package instructions; drain. Combine with soup, eggs, mayonnaise, onion, salt and pepper; mix well. Stir in cheese. Pour into greased soufflé dish. Place soufflé dish in pan filled with 1 inch warm water in oven. Bake at 375° for 1 hour and 10 minutes or till knife inserted in center comes out clean. Yields 8 servings.

C.E. Walton, Douglasville Council (Lawfully Good Eating)

Easy Hash Brown Casserole

1 (10¾-ounce) can cream of chicken soup

1 (16-ounce) carton Dean's onion dip

1 (8-ounce) carton fat-free sour cream

4 cups shredded sharp Cheddar cheese

1 (2-pound) bag frozen cubed hash browns

Salt and pepper to taste

TOPPING: (OPTIONAL)

2 cups crushed cornflakes   ¾ cup butter, melted

Preheat oven to 350°. Combine soup, dip, sour cream, and cheese; add potatoes. Spray 9x13-inch casserole dish with Pam. Add potato mixture. Put Topping on potato mixture, if desired. Bake 1½ hours at 350°.

Susan Sloan, Fayetteville, GA (Great Southern Recipes)

Potato Casserole

4 medium potatoes, cooked, peeled

1 cup milk

½ teaspoon salt

2 cups shredded Cheddar cheese, divided

2 teaspoons finely chopped green onion tops

5 slices bacon, cooked, crumbled

Mash potatoes; set aside. Scald milk; add salt, 1 cup cheese, and onion, stirring till cheese is melted. Add milk mixture and bacon to potatoes; blend well. Spoon mixture into greased 1-quart casserole dish; sprinkle with remaining cheese. Bake at 350° for 10 minutes or till cheese melts. Makes 4–6 servings.

Libby Smith, Atlanta, GA (Great Southern Recipes)

Party Potatoes

6 large potatoes
2 cups sour cream
1 cup margarine, melted
2 (10¾-ounce) cans cream of
  chicken soup

1 small bunch green onions,
  chopped
2 cups shredded Cheddar cheese,
  divided
Salt and pepper to taste

Boil unpeeled potatoes in water to cover in saucepan till tender; drain. Chill overnight. Remove peel; slice thinly. Arrange in baking dish. Combine sour cream, margarine, soup, green onions, 1½ cups cheese, salt and pepper; mix well. Pour over potatoes. Sprinkle with remaining cheese. Bake at 350° till hot and bubbly. Yields 10–12 servings.

Donna Barfield, Macon Council (Lawfully Good Eating);
Ellen C. Fowler, W.E.-Region (Dogwood Delights)

Sweet Potatoes with Orange Sauce

3–4 medium sweet potatoes,
  cooked
½ cup sugar
½ cup light brown sugar

½ cup orange juice
¼ cup butter
2 tablespoons cornstarch
Dash of salt

Peel and slice potatoes; place in glass casserole dish. In saucepan, heat remaining ingredients till thickened. Pour over sweet potatoes. Bake at 350° about 30 minutes.

Annabelle C. Murden, Decatur, GA (Great Southern Recipes)

Sweet Potato Fries

3 sweet potatoes
2 cups oil

Sea salt
Horseradish dip or wasabi mayo

Peel sweet potatoes and cut in long slices the size of French fry strips. Fry sweet potatoes in boiling oil. Drain on paper towels. Roll in sea salt and dip. Great with wrap sandwiches.

Martha Jung LM, Buford, GA (Great Southern Recipes)

Sweet Potato Soufflé

3 cups mashed sweet potatoes
1 cup sugar
½ cup plus ⅓ cup margarine,
  melted, divided
2 eggs, beaten
½ cup milk

1 teaspoon vanilla
⅓ cup self-rising flour
1 cup packed brown sugar
1 cup chopped nuts
1 cup flaked coconut

Combine sweet potatoes, sugar, ½ cup margarine, eggs, milk, and vanilla in large bowl; mix well. Spoon into greased baking dish. Combine remaining ⅓ cup margarine, flour, brown sugar, nuts, and coconut in small bowl; mix well. Sprinkle over sweet potato mixture. Bake at 375° for 25 minutes, or till golden brown. Yields 6–8 servings.

*Virginia Stembridge, Macon Council (Lawfully Good Eating);
Jennifer Strange, Long Lines-AT&T; Sandra Blackwell, Area
(Dogwood Delights); Libby Smith, Atlanta, GA; Mrs. Annie Bradley,
Brookwood-Downtown (Great Southern Recipes)*

Vidalia Onion Pie Casserole

5 medium Vidalia or sweet   Grated Parmesan cheese
  onions, sliced thin   Ritz Crackers, crushed
1 stick margarine

Sauté onions in margarine till limp, but not brown; set aside. Place half the onions in a casserole dish; sprinkle with Parmesan cheese generously. Sprinkle cracker crumbs over cheese; repeat layers. Bake in 325° oven till light brown, about 20 minutes.

Note: May add 2–3 tablespoons milk during baking if too much liquid has been absorbed.

Mary Townsend, Chamblee-North Fulton (Dogwood Delights)

Grilled Sweet Vidalia Onions

4 Vidalia onions   ¼ cup butter
2 tablespoons Worcestershire   Salt and pepper to taste

Remove tops and skins from onions. Cut an "X" halfway through each onion. Brush with Worcestershire; dot with butter and sprinkle with salt and pepper. Wrap each onion in heavy-duty aluminum foil; seal. Place over hot coals and grill 45–50 minutes or till tender, turning occasionally. Onions may be oven roasted at 350° for 1–1½ hours or till tender.

Pete Keel, Conyers, GA (Great Southern Recipes)

Sweet Vidalia Onion Pie Supreme

3 cups thinly sliced Vidalia
  onions
3 tablespoons butter, melted
1 pie shell, baked
½ cup milk

½ cup sour cream, divided
2 eggs, well beaten
1 teaspoon salt
3 tablespoons flour
Bacon slices, fried, crumbled

Cook onions in butter till lightly browned; spoon into pastry shell. Combine milk, ¼ cup sour cream, eggs, and salt. Blend flour with remaining ¼ cup sour cream; combine with egg mixture; pour over onion mixture. Bake in slow 325° oven for 30 minutes or till firm in center. Garnish with crumbled bacon.

Pete Keel, Conyers, GA (Great Southern Recipes)

Vidalia Onion Casserole

¼ cup margarine
¼ cup all-purpose flour
2 cups milk

½ teaspoon salt
2 cups grated Cheddar cheese
6 medium Vidalia onions, sliced

Melt butter. Blend in flour; add milk, slowly stirring till thickened. Add salt and cheese. Pour over sliced onions. Bake, uncovered, 1 hour at 350°.

Arlene T. Davis, Decatur-Tucker (Dogwood Delights II)

Sausage Stuffed Vidalia Onions

4 large Vidalia onions, peeled,
  cored, reserve centers
½–¾ pound pork sausage
½–¾ cup sliced mushrooms
4 ounces herb stuffing mix
  crumbs

⅛ teaspoon thyme
⅛ teaspoon sage
2–4 tablespoons mayonnaise
1 cup grated Cheddar cheese, or
  ½ cup grated fresh Parmesan
  cheese

Place cored onions in a vegetable steamer, or steam in shallow water till barely soft; drain; set aside. Chop reserved onion centers (approximately 1 cup) and sauté with sausage and mushrooms. Drain well on brown paper. Combine sausage mixture with stuffing, herbs, and just enough mayonnaise to moisten stuffing. Spoon stuffing into onions, heaping it about ½ inch above top.

Place filled onions in a greased, shallow baking pan. Bake in preheated 350° oven 20–25 minutes. Top with your choice of cheese and bake an additional 5 minutes or till cheese melts or turns golden. Serves 4.

Note: When coring onions, leave 2 or 3 layers of onions to form a solid shell. Trim base so onions will sit flat.

Bev Brodie, Area (Dogwood Delights II)

An exchange is a practical means of communicating between many people who have telephones. The first known exchange linking two major cities was established between New York and Boston in 1883.

Creamed Corn

2 cups corn (4–6 ears)
2 tablespoons butter
½–1 cup milk

2 tablespoons flour
1 tablespoon sugar
Salt and pepper to taste

Cut corn off cob, slicing tips of kernels with first cut, rest of kernel with next cut. Scrape cob with back of knife to get remainder. Melt butter in skillet. Add corn and reduce heat to low.

Add ½ cup milk and flour. Stir mixture with whisk. Allow to simmer 5 minutes. If too thick, add more milk; if too liquid, add more flour. Stir in sugar, salt and pepper, and serve. Extra sweet corn will not require any additional sugar.

Dorothy Fulcher, Decatur, GA (Great Southern Recipes)

Shoepeg Corn Casserole

1 (14-ounce) can shoepeg corn
1 (10¾-ounce) can cream of
   celery soup
1 (15-ounce) can French-style
   green beans
½ cup grated Cheddar cheese
1 cup sour cream

¼ cup chopped green bell
   pepper
½ cup chopped onion
½ cup chopped celery
Salt and pepper to taste
1 stick margarine, melted
1 stack Ritz Crackers, crushed

Mix all ingredients except margarine and cracker crumbs in a greased casserole dish. Mix melted margarine and cracker crumbs; spread over top of veggie mixture. Bake at 350° for 30 minutes.

Valleria Lowery, Jonesboro-South Fulton (Dogwood Delights II)

Corn-Cheese Casserole

2 (15-ounce) cans whole-kernel
  corn, drained
1½ cups shredded medium
  Cheddar cheese, divided
1 (2-ounce) jar chopped
  pimentos, drained
¼ cup chopped onion

2 tablespoons all-purpose flour
2 tablespoons sugar
1 teaspoon salt
2 eggs, slightly beaten
½ cup milk
2 tablespoons margarine, melted

Combine corn, 1 cup cheese, pimentos, and onion; mix well. Add flour, sugar, salt, eggs, milk, and margarine, stirring to mix. Pour into greased 1½-quart baking dish. Bake at 350° for 40 minutes. Sprinkle with remaining ½ cup cheese. Bake 5 minutes longer. Yields 6 servings.

Shirley Thaxton, Athens-Gainesville Council
(Lawfully Good Eating)

Mother's Squash Dressing

½ cup chopped celery
½ cup chopped onion
½ cup chopped green bell
  pepper
1 stick margarine
1 (10¾-ounce) can cream of
  chicken soup

2 cups cooked squash (about 2
  pounds)
Salt and pepper to taste
2 cups crumbled cooked
  cornbread

Sauté celery, onion, and green pepper in margarine. Mix all ingredients and place in casserole dish. Bake at 350° for 25–30 minutes.

Mittie Keefe, General (Dogwood Delights II)

Squash Casserole

2 cups cooked squash
½ stick butter, softened
1 teaspoon sugar
1 egg, beaten
½ cup grated Cheddar cheese
1 small onion, diced small

½ cup mayonnaise
¼ cup sour cream
1 sleeve Ritz Crackers, crushed,
 mixed with ½ stick melted
 butter

Mix everything together except Ritz Crackers. Place in 2-quart casserole dish. Sprinkle buttered cracker crumbs over squash mixture. Bake at 350° for 35–40 minutes.

Nancy Edenfield, Covington, GA (Great Southern Recipes)

Aunt Fanny's Cabin Squash

3 pounds crookneck squash
½ cup chopped onion
2 eggs, beaten
1 stick butter, divided
1 tablespoon sugar

1 teaspoon salt
½ teaspoon black pepper
½ cup cracker meal or bread
 crumbs

Boil squash till tender; drain thoroughly, then mash. Add onion, eggs, ½ stick butter (melted), sugar, salt, and pepper. Place mixture in greased baking dish. Melt remaining ½ stick butter and pour on top. Sprinkle with cracker meal or bread crumbs. Bake 1 hour at 375°.

Gene Singley, Brookwood-Downtown (Dogwood Delights)

Fried Cabbage

1 small head cabbage
½ cup water

Salt and pepper to taste
1 stick butter

Chop cabbage; wash, and drain well. Place in skillet with water, salt, pepper, and butter. Cover and cook over low heat till tender. Watch carefully to avoid burning. More water can be added, if needed. Serve hot.

Libby Smith, Atlanta, GA (Great Southern Recipes)

Low-Cal Cabbage

½–1 pound ground beef
1 head cabbage, grated
1 or 2 medium onions, grated

1 (10¾-ounce) can tomato soup
½ cup water

Brown beef in skillet; drain. Mix cabbage and onion together; layer with ground beef till all used up in casserole dish. Mix tomato soup with water; pour on top. Bake at 350° for 1 hour.

Mack Henderson, Austell-Marietta (Dogwood Delights II)

Green Bean Casserole

2 (9-ounce) packages frozen
 green beans, thawed, drained
1 (10¾-ounce) can cream of
 mushroom soup

¾ cup milk
⅛ teaspoon pepper
1 (3-ounce) can French fried
 onions, divided

Combine green beans, soup, milk, pepper, and half the onions; mix well. Pour into 1½-quart baking dish. Bake at 350° for 30 minutes. Top with remaining onions. Bake till golden. Yields 6 servings.

Linda Kite, Macon Council (Lawfully Good Eating)

Eggplant Casserole

2 cups cubed, peeled eggplant   ¾ cup milk
1½ teaspoons salt, divided   2 eggs, beaten
1 tablespoon butter   12 saltine crackers, crushed
1½ cups shredded cheese

Cook eggplant in water to cover with 1 teaspoon salt till tender; drain. Mash in bowl till smooth. Add butter and cheese, stirring till cheese is melted. Combine milk, eggs, remaining ½ teaspoon salt, and crackers in small bowl. Stir into eggplant mixture. Pour into 1½-quart baking dish. Bake at 400° for 30 minutes. Yields 4 servings.

Mary E. Mallory, Athens-Gainesville Council
(Lawfully Good Eating)

Fried Cauliflower

1 large cauliflower   ½ teaspoon garlic salt
2 eggs   ½ cup Romano cheese
½ cup milk   1 tablespoon parsley
½ cup all-purpose flour   3 cups oil for frying
1 cup bread crumbs

Wash and separate flowerets. Combine eggs, milk, and flour; beat till smooth. In large bowl, combine bread crumbs, garlic salt, Romano cheese, and parsley. Dip flowerets into batter, then into dry combined ingredients. Fry till golden brown. Drain on paper towels. Serve hot or at room temperature.

Carolyn Alvaro, Chamblee-North Fulton (Dogwood Delights)

Copper Penny Carrots

2 pounds carrots
¼ cup water
1 medium purple onion, sliced
1 (10-ounce) package frozen
  peas
1 small green bell pepper,
  sliced
1 (10¾-ounce) can tomato soup

½ cup oil
1 cup sugar
¾ cup cider vinegar
1 teaspoon prepared mustard
½ teaspoon salt
1 teaspoon Worcestershire
¼ teaspoon pepper

Peel and slice carrots. Place in medium saucepan with water.
Cover and cook till crisp-tender, about 5 minutes; do not overcook.
Rinse under cold water to stop cooking. Drain and cool. Separate
onion slices into rings in medium bowl. Alternate layers of cooked
carrots, peas, onion rings, and green pepper. In another medium
bowl, mix remaining ingredients till smooth. Pour over vegetables. Cover and refrigerate overnight. May be refrigerated up to
2 weeks. Serves 8.

E. Banovatz, Brookwood-Downtown (Dogwood Delights)

Lemon-Glazed Carrots

1 pound carrots, sliced
  diagonally into 1-inch pieces
Salt to taste

3 tablespoons butter
2 tablespoons sugar
4 thin slices lemon

Cook carrots in saucepan with enough salted water to cover 15
minutes, or till tender; drain. Melt butter in large skillet. Stir in
sugar. Add lemon slices and carrots. Cook over medium heat till
carrots are glazed, stirring occasionally. Yields 4 servings.

Maureen Middleton, Athens-Gainesville Council
(Lawfully Good Eating)

Spinach Artichoke Casserole

2 (10-ounce) packages frozen
  chopped spinach
2 (15-ounce) cans artichokes,
  drained
1 (8-ounce) package cream
  cheese, softened

1 stick butter
2 tablespoons lemon juice
1 (3½-ounce) can French fried
  onions

Cook spinach; drain well. Cut artichokes in half and put in bottom of small casserole dish. Mix cream cheese, butter, lemon juice, and drained spinach. Spread mixture over artichokes and place in 350° oven. Let heat till cream cheese bubbles, about 20 minutes. Remove from oven and sprinkle French fried onions on top. Put back in oven till onions are crisp.

Jerry Farkas, Marietta, GA (Great Southern Recipes)

Tomato Pudding Casserole

1 cup brown sugar (do not pack)
½ teaspoon salt
1 (10-ounce) can chopped
  tomatoes

1 cup bread cubes
½ stick butter, melted

Combine sugar, salt, and tomatoes in saucepan. Boil 5 minutes. In a greased casserole dish, place bread cubes; pour melted butter over cubes. Add tomato mixture; place cover on casserole and bake 30 minutes at 350°.

Janeen B. Aylor, Blairsville, GA (Great Southern Recipes)

Edie's Baked Beans

1 (28-ounce) can pork and
   beans
½ cup ketchup
¼ cup mustard
1 pound ground chuck or
   ground turkey
1 cup brown sugar

½ onion, diced
½ green bell pepper, diced
½ red bell pepper, diced
1 (8-ounce) can crushed
   pineapple
½ pound beef bacon, cooked,
   crumbled

Combine all ingredients except pineapple and bacon together and bake at 350° for 1 hour. Let cool. Sprinkle pineapple and bacon on top. Serve.

Edith M. Browning, Decatur-Tucker (Dogwood Delights II)

Baked Beans

1 (16-ounce) can pork and
   beans
¼ cup ketchup
¼ cup chili sauce
½ teaspoon dry mustard

2 tablespoons molasses
2 tablespoons brown sugar
1 onion, chopped fine
Bacon

Mix all ingredients together except bacon, rinsing bean can out with ¼ cup water and adding. Put into well-greased baking dish. Put strips of bacon over top. Bake in 400° oven 45–50 minutes.

Ella L. Callahan, General (Dogwood Delights)

Pasta, Rice, Etc.

1930
Single Handset
Oval-Base

Although the single handset containing both the receiver and transmitter was developed for operators and repairmen by 1878, it wasn't until 1927 that the single handset telephone was introduced to the general public. The 1927 model had a round base. In 1930 it was redesigned with an elongated base made to compliment the long handset. The dial was also recessed into the front of the phone. Like the Candlestick, only the switchhook and switch were contained in the phone. The network and ringer were contained in a subset that was mounted on the wall. The subsets contained a new induction coil that would be used for nearly twenty years.

Macaroni and Cheese

1 (10¾-ounce) can cream of
  mushroom soup
1 cup mayonnaise
¼ cup pimentos
¼ cup grated onion
1 pound grated sharp Cheddar
  cheese

1 (8-ounce) package elbow
  macaroni, cooked, drained
3 tablespoons butter, melted
3 tablespoons cheese crackers,
  crumbled

Combine all ingredients with macaroni except butter and cracker crumbs. Mix butter and crumbs and sprinkle on top. Bake 25 minutes at 325°.

Irene Mooney, Chamblee-North Fulton (Dogwood Delights II)

Deep-Dish Mac and Cheese

1 (1-pound) package elbow
  macaroni
¾ stick butter
1 cup mozzarella cheese
1 cup ricotta cheese

1 (8-ounce) package cream
  cheese
½ cup milk
2 cups shredded Cheddar cheese

Preheat oven to 350°. In large saucepan, boil macaroni to desired consistency. Pour macaroni into 10x13-inch casserole dish. Cut butter into slices and melt in macaroni.

Combine mozzarella, ricotta, cream cheese, and milk in microwave-safe bowl; cover with paper towel. Microwave about 4 minutes, stirring every minute. Once cheese mixture is melted well, pour mixture into macaroni and stir thoroughly. Bake in preheated oven 20 minutes. Remove; sprinkle Cheddar cheese over top and bake another 10 minutes, or till cheese is bubbly.

Christopher Weldon, Marietta, GA (Great Southern Recipes)

Crockpot Macaroni and Cheese

1 (8-ounce) box elbow macaroni
1 stick margarine
2½ cups grated Cheddar
  cheese, divided
1½ cups milk
2 eggs, beaten
1 (12-ounce) can evaporated
  milk
Salt and pepper to taste

Cook and drain macaroni. Put in crockpot. Add margarine and 2 cups cheese; stir. Add milk, beaten eggs, evaporated milk, salt and pepper. Stir together in crockpot. Top with remaining ½ cup cheese and cover. Cook 3 hours on LOW heat.

Lynne Kannaly, Charlotte, NC (Great Southern Recipes)

Roast Beef Casserole

1 box deluxe macaroni and
  cheese
1 medium onion, chopped
1 tablespoon butter
1 (10¾-ounce) can cream of
  mushroom soup
1 (16-ounce) can roast beef and
  gravy

Cook macaroni by itself; drain. Sauté onion in butter till tender. Add macaroni, cheese from macaroni box, soup, and beef. Stir together really well. Pour into lightly greased casserole dish and bake about 25 minutes at 350°.

Lois McKinney, Area (Dogwood Delights)

Chicken and Macaroni

1 (8-ounce) package elbow
  macaroni
3 tablespoons butter
1 small green bell pepper,
  chopped
1 celery stalk, thinly sliced
3 tablespoons all-purpose flour

¾ teaspoon salt
⅛ teaspoon pepper
2 cups milk
1 (5- to 6-ounce) can chunk
  chicken
1 (8-ounce) package shredded
  Cheddar cheese

Prepare macaroni as label directs; drain; keep warm. Meanwhile, in 3-quart saucepan over medium heat, melt butter; add green pepper and celery. Cook till vegetables are tender, stirring occasionally. Stir in flour, salt, and pepper till blended. Gradually stir in milk. Cook, stirring constantly, till sauce is slightly thickened. Gently stir in chicken and cheese, just till cheese is melted. Remove saucepan from heat. Stir cooked hot elbow macaroni into mixture till well blended. Serve with tossed salad.

Kathy Evans, General (Dogwood Delights II)

The very first American 911 call was placed on February 16, 1968, in Haleyville, Alabama. Alabama Speaker of the House, Rankin Fite, made the first call from another city hall room. It was answered by Congressman Tom Bevill on a bright red telephone located in the police department. Bob Gallagher, president of the Alabama Telephone Company initiated and directed the overall 911 effort. Bob Fitzgerald, plant manager, designed and engineered the needed circuitry for the first U.S. 911 system.

Chicken Spaghetti

1 (3- to 4-pound) fryer
7–10 ounces spaghetti
1 (10¾-ounce) can cream of
  mushroom soup
1 (10¾-ounce) can cream of
  chicken soup

1 (12-ounce) can chicken broth
1 teaspoon salt
⅛ teaspoon pepper
1 large onion, chopped
1–1½ cups shredded mild
  Cheddar cheese

Boil fryer till tender; cool; remove meat from bones; cut up. Cook spaghetti according to package directions; drain. Mix soups, broth, salt, pepper, and onion; stir into spaghetti. Stir in chicken pieces and pour mixture into casserole dish. Top with grated cheese. Bake in 350° oven 1 hour.

Evelyn Lingerfelt, Jonesboro-South Fulton (Dogwood Delights)

Chicken Spaghetti

1 onion, chopped
1 green bell pepper, chopped
¾ stick margarine
16 ounces spaghetti
1 fryer, boiled, cut into bite-size
  pieces (reserve broth)
1 pound Velveeta cheese,
  chopped

1 (10-ounce) can Ro-Tel
  tomatoes
1 (2-ounce) jar pimentos
1 (10¾-ounce) can cream of
  mushroom soup

Sauté onion and pepper in margarine. Boil spaghetti in chicken broth; drain. Add Velveeta and remaining ingredients including chicken. Spoon into lightly greased 9x13-inch pan; bake 25 minutes at 350°.

Doris Johnson, Jonesboro-South Fulton (Dogwood Delights II)

Cheese and Pasta in a Pot

2 pounds lean ground beef
2 medium onions, chopped
1 clove garlic, minced
1 (14-ounce) jar spaghetti sauce
1 (14½-ounce) can stewed
  tomatoes
1 (4-ounce) can mushrooms
Salt to taste

8 ounces shell or chariot wheel
  macaroni
1½ pints sour cream
1 (4- to 6-ounce) package
  provolone cheese slices
1 (6- to 8-ounce) package
  mozzarella cheese slices

Brown beef in deep frying pan. Drain; add onions and garlic. Add sauce, tomatoes, and mushrooms. Mix well and salt to taste. Simmer till onions turn yellow. Cook macaroni; drain well. In lightly greased, deep casserole, place layer of macaroni. Cover with half the meat mixture. Spread top with half of sour cream, and cover with slices of Provolone cheese. Repeat, using all ingredients, and finish with mozzarella slices. Cover and bake at 350° for 1 hour. Serves 8.

Beverly Brodie, Area (Dogwood Delights II)

White Lasagna

1 (8-ounce) package lasagna
  noodles
1 pound ground turkey
1 cup chopped celery
¾ cup chopped onion
1–2 garlic cloves, minced
2 teaspoons crushed sweet basil
1 teaspoon oregano
¾ teaspoon salt
½ teaspoon pepper
½ teaspoon Italian herb
  seasoning

1 cup half-and-half
1 (3-ounce) package cream
  cheese
½ cup dry white wine
2 cups shredded Cheddar cheese
1½ cups shredded Gouda
  cheese
1 large egg
12 ounces ricotta, or cottage
  cheese
16 ounces mozzarella cheese,
  sliced, divided

Cook noodles by package directions; set aside. In large skillet, lightly brown ground turkey. Add celery, onion, and garlic; cook till vegetables are tender; drain. Stir in basil, oregano, salt, pepper, and Italian seasoning. Add cream and cream cheese; cook and stir over low heat to melt cheese. Stir in wine. Gradually add Cheddar and Gouda cheeses, stirring till nearly melted. Remove from heat.

In a bowl, slightly beat egg; add ricotta cheese and stir to combine. Layer half the noodles in a greased 9x12-inch baking pan. Top with half the meat sauce, half the ricotta cheese mixture, and half the mozzarella slices. Repeat layers. Bake, uncovered, at 375° for 30–35 minutes. Let stand 10 minutes before serving. Serves 12.

Bill Kent (Great Southern Recipes)

Skillet Lasagna

1 pound ground beef
2 tablespoons butter
1 envelope spaghetti sauce mix
3 cups broad noodles, uncooked
1 (16-ounce) carton cottage
   cheese
2 teaspoons crushed basil

1 tablespoon parsley flakes
1 teaspoon salt
1 (14½-ounce) can tomatoes
1 (8-ounce) can tomato sauce
1 cup water
1 (8-ounce) package shredded
   mozzarella cheese

Cook meat in butter; drain. Sprinkle with ½ spaghetti sauce mix. Top with noodles; cover with cottage cheese. Sprinkle with remaining spaghetti sauce mix, basil, parsley, and salt. Pour tomatoes, tomato sauce, and water over top. Cover and simmer 35 minutes. Sprinkle mozzarella over top and let stand 5 minutes.

Barbara Smith, Austell-Marietta (Dogwood Delights II)

Baked Spaghetti

1 pound ground meat
1 (26-ounce) jar spaghetti sauce
1 envelope spaghetti sauce mix
1 (8-ounce) can tomatoes or
   tomato sauce

1 teaspoon garlic powder
½ pound spaghetti, cooked

Brown meat; drain. Add sauce, sauce mix, tomatoes, garlic and cooked spaghetti. Put in greased baking dish and cook in 300° oven 30 minutes.

Mary Jo Rainey, General (Dogwood Delights II)

Fettucini Alfredo

½ cup butter, softened
¼ cup whipping cream (room temperature)

½ cup grated Parmesan cheese
1 (16-ounce) package fettucini, cooked

Cream butter; beat in cream, a little at a time, till mixture is well combined. Beat in Parmesan cheese. Set aside till room temperature. Serve over cooked fettucini.

Lisa Cubbon, Austell-Marietta (Dogwood Delights II)

Linguine Genoese Pesto

½ cup olive oil
1 tablespoon dried basil
2 large cloves garlic, very finely minced
¼ cup freshly grated Parmesan cheese

2 tablespoons grated Romano cheese
2 tablespoons toasted pine nuts
¼ teaspoon salt
1 pound linguine pasta
4 tablespoons butter

In small saucepan, heat olive oil and basil over a very low flame, about 5 minutes. In well of electric blender, put oil with basil, garlic, Parmesan cheese, Romano cheese, pinenuts, and salt. Blend at high speed 30 seconds. Cook linguine pasta in boiling, salted water just till tender; drain well. Pour sauce over linguine on large platter. Add butter and toss thoroughly to blend sauce, butter, and linguine. Serves 4.

Robert Cornelia, W. E.-BTL/Cable (Dogwood Delights)

Italian Sausage Linguine

2 teaspoons olive oil
2 garlic cloves, minced
1 pound Italian sausage
2 (14½-ounce) cans diced
   seasoned tomatoes
1 cup chopped fresh basil

½ cup chopped green onions
1 teaspoon oregano
Black pepper to taste
4 cups cooked linguine
½ cup chopped fresh parsley
   (optional)

Heat olive oil in nonstick frying pan over low heat; add minced garlic and sauté 5 minutes. Increase heat to medium and add sausage. Break sausage into small pieces as it browns. Once sausage is fully cooked, stir in tomatoes, basil, green onions, and oregano. Add pepper to taste. Simmer another 15 minutes, allowing mixture to thicken. Pour sauce over cooked linguine and sprinkle with fresh parsley, if desired.

Lynn Hull (Great Southern Recipes)

Onion Rice

1 medium onion, chopped
1 cup rice

2 (10-ounce) cans beef consommé
1 stick butter

Put all ingredients in covered casserole dish; mix well. Bake at 350° for 1 hour and 15 minutes, or till it begins to turn brown around edges.

Bill Easterling, General (Dogwood Delights II)

Rice Pilaf

¼ cup chopped onion
¼ cup chopped celery
¼ cup chopped green bell
  pepper
2 tablespoons butter
1 cup hot water

1 (4-ounce) can sliced
  mushrooms, drained
⅓ cup uncooked long-grain
  rice
1 tablespoon instant chicken
  bouillon

In 1-quart casserole dish, combine onion, celery, green pepper, and butter. Microwave on HIGH for 4–6½ minutes, till vegetables are tender crisp.

Stir in remaining ingredients; cover. Microwave at HIGH for 6½ minutes. Reduce power to MEDIUM-HIGH and microwave 10–12 minutes till liquid is absorbed. Let stand, covered, 10 minutes. Fluff with fork before serving. Makes 2–3 servings.

Betty McDilda, Central (Dogwood Delights II)

Saffron Rice Pilaf

½ cup finely chopped onion
1 clove garlic, minced
⅓ cup butter
2 cups rice
1 tablespoon chopped parsley
2 teaspoons saffron

¼ teaspoon leaf thyme
⅛ teaspoon pepper
½ bay leaf
2 teaspoons salt
2 (14-ounce) cans chicken broth
1½ cups water

Cook onion and garlic in butter till tender, not brown, in 2-quart Dutch oven. Stir in rice; heat. Mix in all seasonings. Combine chicken broth and water in saucepan; bring to a boil. Pour over rice dish. Cover. Bake in 350° oven till liquid is absorbed (about 30 minutes). Serves 8.

Leola R. Farmer, Jonesboro-South Fulton (Dogwood Delights)

Posey Fried Rice

1 cup long-grain white rice
2 teaspoons salt, divided
Oil
2 teaspoons paprika
2 eggs, beaten
½ cup shrimp
1 cup thinly sliced chicken
  breast
½ cup finely chopped country
  ham

3 green onions, chopped
½ cup grated carrots
½ cup sliced mushrooms
Frozen peas
Light soy sauce to taste
Dash of sesame oil
MSG (optional)
Salt and pepper to taste

Wash rice well under running water. Bring a pan full of water to a boil; add 1 teaspoon salt, a couple drops of cooking oil, and rice. Slowly bring back to a boil and then boil exactly 10 minutes. Drain and leave to cool. When cool, add paprika to rice; mix well. Have all ingredients prepared and ready to add.

Bring a wok to smoking hot; add 1 tablespoon oil and any of the meats that you wish to use. Fry 5–6 minutes. Remove from wok; lightly oil wok and fry eggs till just set (like an omelet). Remove from wok. Remove any residue from wok with paper towels; reheat wok to very hot and add 2 tablespoons oil. Add rice; cook till heated through, stirring constantly. Add meat, onions, carrots, mushrooms, and peas. Chop eggs and add to rice; stir till heated through. Add light soy sauce, if desired. Add sesame oil, MSG, if desired, and salt and pepper to taste.

Em Posey (Great Southern Recipes)

Skillet Fried Rice

3 cups uncooked rice
6 tablespoons oil
5 eggs, beaten
6 tablespoons soy sauce
¼ teaspoon garlic powder
2 onions, chopped
2 cups diagonally sliced celery

Cook rice as package directs; allow to cool. Heat oil in large skillet; pour in eggs. Cut up eggs with 2 knives. Add soy sauce and garlic powder. Add rice, onions, and celery. Stir over low heat 3–5 minutes. Makes 12–14 servings.

Jean Roan, Austell-Marietta (Dogwood Delights II)

Rice Brennen

1 cup dry rice
1 (10¾-ounce) can onion soup
1 soup can water
1 (4-ounce) can sliced
   mushrooms
½ stick butter, melted

Combine all ingredients. Pour into greased casserole dish; cover with foil. Bake 1 hour at 300°.

Sarah R. Davis, General (Dogwood Delights)

Spanish Rice

1 (15-ounce) can tomato sauce
2 (14-ounce) cans chicken broth
Salt and pepper to taste
Oregano to taste
2 cups long-grain rice
½ cup chopped red onion

Heat tomato sauce, chicken broth, salt, pepper, and oregano in a saucepan. Brown rice and onion in large frying pan; pour heated broth mixture over. Put a couple pats of butter in and cover. Cook on low heat 20–25 minutes.

Linda Clabaugh, Blue Ridge, GA (Great Southern Recipes)

Red Rice

2 slices bacon, cut into ½-inch
  pieces
⅔ cup chopped onion
1 teaspoon dried thyme leaves
1 green bell pepper, chopped
1 or 2 jalapeño peppers,
  seeded, chopped
1 (14-ounce) can tomato purée
  (or 2 cups fresh)
1 tablespoon brown sugar
2 cups cold water
2 cups uncooked rice
1 cup small pieces cooked ham

Cook bacon in heavy-bottomed saucepan till crisp. Remove bacon pieces from pan; set aside. Add onions to pan; stir and simmer a few minutes. Stir in thyme, green and hot peppers, tomato purée, brown sugar, water, rice, ham, and reserved bacon. Mix well.

Transfer mixture to a microwave-safe 2-quart casserole. Cook on HIGH 5 minutes, then on MEDIUM for 20–25 minutes. Let set 5 minutes before stirring.

Note: May use 4 cups cooked rice, omitting water and changing cooking time to 10 minutes on HIGH.

Joann G. Thornton, General (Dogwood Delights II)

Almond Rice Casserole

4 cups uncooked white rice
8 cups water
½ cup butter
2 (10¾-ounce) cans cream of
  mushroom soup

1 (4-ounce) can sliced
  mushrooms
1 cup slivered almonds
2 cups shredded cheese, divided

Preheat oven to 350°. In large saucepan, bring water to a boil. Add rice and stir. Reduce heat; cover and simmer 20 minutes.

Meanwhile, in saucepan over medium heat, melt butter and stir in soup. Combine soup mixture with cooked rice; stir in mushrooms and almonds. Mix well. Spoon half the mixture into a greased 1½-quart casserole dish. Sprinkle half the cheese over, then repeat layers. Bake 20 minutes or till cheese is melted. Serves 4–6.

Sherry Scott (Great Southern Recipes)

Monterey Rice

2 (4-ounce) cans chopped green
  chiles
2 cups sour cream

1 cup rice, cooked
12 ounces Monterey Jack cheese,
  sliced

Combine chiles and sour cream in bowl; mix well. Spread ⅓ rice in buttered 10x10-inch baking dish. Layer sour cream mixture, cheese, and remaining rice, ½ at a time, in prepared dish. Bake at 350° for 30 minutes. Yields 4 servings.

Carol C. Tully, Henry County Sheriff's Department
(Lawfully Good Eating)

Cheeseburger Pie

1 cup tomato sauce, no sugar
  added
½ cup diced onion
½ medium green bell pepper,
  diced
1 packet instant beef broth and
  seasoning mix
1 teaspoon sugar
½ teaspoon chili powder
¼ teaspoon garlic powder
½ pound ground beef, cooked,
  crumbled
1 cup grated Cheddar cheese,
  divided
2 cups cooked rice

Preheat oven to 375°. In medium saucepan, combine first 7 ingredients. Simmer 8–10 minutes, or till vegetables are tender. Add beef, ¾ of cheese, and rice; stir till cheese melts. Turn into an 8x8-inch pan treated with nonstick spray. Sprinkle with remaining cheese. Bake ½ hour. Remove from oven; allow to sit 10–15 minutes before cutting. Serves 4.

Sandra Holcomb, Jonesboro, South Fulton (Dogwood Delights)

Pizza Rice

½ teaspoon oregano
½ cup tomato sauce
1 tablespoon butter
1½ cups water
Salt and pepper to taste
1 cup Minute Rice
1 cup grated Cheddar cheese

Combine all ingredients except rice and cheese in saucepan. Bring to a boil; remove from heat. Add rice and cheese. Stir; let sit 5 minutes. Serves 4.

C. Hedrick, General (Dogwood Delights)

Dirty Rice

1 onion, chopped
1 clove garlic, minced
½ stick butter
½ pound hamburger (or chicken giblets)
1¼ cups raw rice
1 (8-ounce) can mushroom sauce
1 can water
1 (10-ounce) can beef consommé
Red pepper to taste
1 tablespoon Worcestershire

Sauté onion and garlic in butter. Add meat and cook till no longer red; drain. Add rice, sauce, water, consommé, red pepper, and Worcestershire. Pour into greased casserole dish; bake, covered, about 1 hour at 350°.

Vivian Van Cleave, Long Lines-AT&T Communications
(Dogwood Delights)

Chicken and Rice

2½–3 cups raw rice
3 cups water
1 (10¾-ounce) can cream of onion soup, or French onion soup
1 (10¾-ounce) can cream of mushroom or chicken soup
⅔ pound chicken pieces
Salt and pepper to taste

Mix rice, water, and soups together. Pour into greased 9x13-inch baking dish. Sprinkle chicken with salt and pepper; place on top of rice mixture. Bake at 350° for 1 hour and 15 minutes. Turn chicken about halfway through cooking. Add more water, if needed.

Edna Whaley, Austell-Marietta (Dogwood Delights)

Chicken and Wild Rice

1 (10¾-ounce) can cream of
  celery soup
1½ cups chicken stock
½ cup mayonnaise
1 package wild and long-grain
  rice
2–3 cups cooked, diced chicken

1 (15-ounce) can French-style
  green beans, well drained
1 (2-ounce) jar chopped
  pimentos, well drained
1 medium onion, chopped
1 (8-ounce) can sliced water
  chestnuts, well drained

Mix soup, stock, mayonnaise, and flavor packet from rice; set aside. In large casserole dish, layer remaining ingredients. Pour soup mixture over layers. Bake, uncovered, 40–45 minutes at 375°.

Marilyn Guyton, Austell-Marietta (Dogwood Delights)

Chicken Rice 'n Spice

1 chicken, cut into pieces
1 teaspoon salt

1 bay leaf
1 (8-ounce) box herb rice

Boil chicken till tender in water with salt and bay leaf. Cool, cut chicken into bite-size pieces; set aside. Cook herb rice according to package directions. Set aside.

SAUCE:

1 (10¾-ounce) can cream of
  chicken soup
½ (5-ounce) can evaporated
  milk

⅔ cup mayonnaise
½ cup grated Cheddar cheese
1 teaspoon lemon juice
1 tablespoon curry powder

Combine all ingredient in saucepan; cook over medium heat till cheese melts. In greased 9x13-inch baking dish, layer all the rice and chicken; pour Sauce over top. Bake at 325° for 30–40 minutes, or till lightly golden brown.

Mary Kay Buschman, Chamblee-North Fulton
(Dogwood Delights)

Chili on Rice

Brown rice tastes nutty and goes very well with chili. Brown rice takes longer to cook than white rice; so allow enough time to cook properly.

3 teaspoons olive oil
1 medium onion, diced
1 clove garlic, diced
½ cup red bell pepper, diced
1 large carrot, diced
½ tablespoon chili powder
1 teaspoon ground cumin
1 (14½-ounce) can chopped
   tomatoes

1 cup chicken broth
2 (15-ounce) cans black beans
Kernels from 1 ear fresh corn
Coarse salt and ground pepper
   to taste
2 cups brown rice
Grated Cheddar cheese
Tortilla chips

Heat oil in large pot. Sauté onion 5–10 minutes (do not brown), then add garlic, pepper, and carrot. Add chili powder and cumin; cook without liquids 10 minutes. Add tomatoes, broth, and beans. Bring to a boil for 5–10 minutes. Add corn and turn heat down to medium-low. Add salt and pepper to taste. Simmer 15 minutes or longer. Cook brown rice according to package instructions.

Place ¼ cup cooked rice in each bowl. Add chili, and sprinkle grated cheese on top. Serve with tortilla chips. Serves 4–5.

Martha Jung LM, Buford, GA (Great Southern Recipes)

Smoked Sausage Jambalaya

1–1½ pounds smoked sausage
1 tablespoon cooking oil
4 green onions, chopped
½ green bell pepper, minced
3 cloves garlic, minced
½ onion, chopped
1 cup long-grain uncooked rice
2 cups water
Salt and pepper to taste

Remove skin from sausage and slice in small pieces. In skillet, brown sausage in oil; remove. Cook green onions, green pepper, garlic, and onion in oil. Reduce heat; add sausage, rice, water, and seasonings. Cover and cook slowly till rice is done, about 20 minutes. Stir carefully once or twice during cooking.

Mrs. Louis W. Henderson, General (Dogwood Delights)

Sausage and Wild Rice Casserole

1 pound hot sausage
1 box Uncle Ben's wild rice
1 (10¾-ounce) can cream of
  mushroom soup
1 (10¾-ounce) can cream of
  celery soup
1 cup chopped onion
1 cup chopped green bell pepper
1 cup chopped celery

Brown sausage; drain. Cook rice according to package directions. Mix all ingredients; pour into greased casserole dish. Bake at 350° for 45–60 minutes.

Jane Bridges, Area (Dogwood Delights II)

Meats

1937
"300" Series

An innovation in telephone design was the placing of the bell in the base of the "300" Series desk set. The "300" Series was the first model that included the ringer, coil, and capacitor in the base, forming a complete phone in one package. Previous models required an external subset that contained these components. The "300" Series was made from 1936 until 1954. Earlier versions had housings made of die-cast metal but thermo-plastic was substituted in the early 1940s due to the onset of World War II.

Soon crossbar switching was introduced, and automation came to long-distance switching. Dialed routing codes soon gave way to the familiar area codes, which the switch itself could translate into the needed routing information. Call completion time dropped to 10–20 seconds.

Country Pie

CRUST:

1 pound ground beef
¼ (8-ounce) can tomato sauce
⅛ teaspoon pepper
½ cup chopped onion

1½ teaspoons salt
½ teaspoon oregano
½ cup bread crumbs

Combine all ingredients and press into a 9-inch pie pan.

FILLING:

1½ (8-ounce) cans tomato
  sauce
1 cup water

1⅓ cups Minute Rice
1 teaspoon salt
1 cup grated Cheddar cheese

Combine ingredients and put in Crust. Bake at 350° for 25 minutes. Top with more grated cheese and bake 10 minutes more. Bake with large pan underneath to catch overflow.

Pam Sampler, Austell-Marietta (Dogwood Delights II)

Hamburger Pie

1 pound hamburger meat
1 medium onion, chopped
1 (15-ounce) can cut green
  beans, drained

1 (10¾-ounce) can tomato soup
4 slices Cheddar cheese
4 medium potatoes, boiled,
  drained, creamed

Brown hamburger meat and onion; when done, add beans and soup; mix well. Layer in a casserole with cheese and potatoes. Make sure potatoes cover the entire contents. Bake at 350° till you see it bubbling around the sides.

Betty Revis, Central (Dogwood Delights II)

Southern Meat Pies

1 pound ground chuck	4–5 cloves garlic, chopped
1 pound ground pork or turkey	1 tablespoon flour
1 medium onion, chopped	1 teaspoon salt
1 bunch green onions with tops, chopped	¼–½ teaspoon red pepper
	½ teaspoon black pepper

Brown meat in skillet, stirring till crumbly; remove meat with slotted spoon, reserving drippings in skillet. Add onion, green onions, and garlic to skillet. Sauté till tender. Stir in flour, salt, red pepper, and black pepper. Return meat to skillet; mix well; set aside.

DOUGH:

8 cups all-purpose flour	2 eggs, beaten
2 teaspoons baking powder	2¼ cups milk
4 teaspoons salt	Oil for frying
1 cup shortening	

Mix flour, baking powder, and salt in bowl. Cut in shortening till crumbly. Add mixture of eggs and milk gradually, mixing with fork to form dough. Divide into 4 portions. Roll on floured surface. Cut each portion into 5 circles, using saucer as guide. Place about ¼ cup meat mixture onto each circle. Fold circles over to enclose filling; press edges with fork to seal. Fry in 3 inches oil in skillet till brown on both sides. Serve with tomato-onion relish. May freeze and thaw in refrigerator overnight before frying, if desired. Yields 10 meat pies.

Lucy Parmer, Columbus Council (Lawfully Good Eating)

Shepherd's Pie

8 medium potatoes
½ stick butter
½ cup milk
Salt and pepper to taste
1½ pounds ground beef

1 large onion, chopped
1 tablespoon Worcestershire
2 (15-ounce) cans creamed corn, divided
Pats of butter

Boil and mash potatoes with butter, milk, salt and pepper. In heavy skillet, combine beef, onion, and Worcestershire. Cook till beef is browned and onions are transparent.

In deep casserole, layer ingredients, beginning with beef mixture; add 1½ cans corn, then potatoes. Pour remaining corn over potatoes. Dot corn with butter. Bake at 350° for 30 minutes. Serves 8–10.

Sara Davis, General (Dogwood Delights II)

Beef Casserole

2 pounds ground beef
1 onion, chopped
4 (10¼-ounce) cans spaghetti sauce

1 pound fine noodles, cooked
1 pound shredded sharp Cheddar cheese

Cook meat and onion in skillet; drain; add sauce and heat. In casserole dish, arrange half the noodles, half the sauce, half the cheese. Repeat for second layer, ending with cheese. Bake in 350° oven till cheese is melted.

Sheila Hull, Area (Dogwood Delights II)

Beef Roll

1 clove garlic, finely sliced
1 teaspoon grated Parmesan
  cheese
1 hard-boiled egg, chopped
½ teaspoon chopped parsley
2 slices bacon, cut into 1-inch
  pieces
1 teaspoon salt, divided

⅜ teaspoon pepper, divided
1 (1½-pound) round steak, ½
  inch thick
1 small onion, sliced
¼ cup olive oil
1 (20-ounce) can tomatoes,
  sieved
1 bay leaf

Combine garlic, cheese, egg, parsley, bacon, ½ teaspoon salt, and ⅛ teaspoon pepper in bowl; mix well. Spread on steak. Roll up steak to enclose filling; tie securely. Sauté onion in olive oil in skillet till tender. Add steak roll; cook till brown on all sides. Combine tomatoes, bay leaf, remaining salt, and remaining pepper in bowl; mix well. Spread over steak. Simmer, covered, 1½ hours, or till done to taste. Discard bay leaf and string. Slice steak roll. Serve with sauce. Yields 4–5 servings.

Margaret Casalino, Augusta Council (Lawfully Good Eating)

Ground Beef Casserole

1 pound ground beef
1 (10¾-ounce) can cream of
  mushroom soup
¼ cup packed brown sugar
¼ cup ketchup
1 onion, chopped

1 (16-ounce) can kidney beans
1 (16-ounce) can French-style
  green beans, drained
4 slices bacon, crisp-fried,
  crumbled

Brown ground beef in saucepan, stirring till crumbly; drain. Add soup, brown sugar, ketchup, and onion; mix well. Fold in beans and bacon. Spoon into 2-quart baking dish. Bake, covered, at 350° for 30 minutes or till heated through. Yields 6 servings.

Lisa Chandler, Athens-Gainesville Council
(Lawfully Good Eating)

Pizza Meatloaf

2 pounds ground beef
1 cup cracker crumbs
½ cup milk
½ cup chopped onion
2 eggs

½ cup grated Parmesan cheese
1 teaspoon oregano
1 (8-ounce) can pizza sauce
1 cup shredded mozzarella

Combine ground beef, cracker crumbs, milk, onion, eggs, Parmesan cheese, and oregano; mix well. Shape into loaf in baking pan. Bake at 350° for 30 minutes. Spread pizza sauce over top. Bake 15 minutes; sprinkle with mozzarella cheese; bake just till cheese melts. Yields 6 servings.

Linda Thompson, Albany Council (Lawfully Good Eating)

Tex-Mex Meatloaf

1 onion, diced
1½ pounds ground sirloin
1 cup soft bread crumbs
1 egg, well beaten
1 (4-ounce) can chopped black
   olives, drained

1 (14½-ounce) can chopped
   tomatoes, drained
½ diced chile pepper
Garlic to taste
Salt and pepper to taste
1 cup shredded Cheddar Cheese

Preheat oven to 350°. Mix all ingredients except cheese and shape into loaf pan. Bake 50–55 minutes. Drain grease from loaf pan several times during cooking. Sprinkle cheese on top; return to oven till cheese melts.

Shannon Hayes, Austell-Marietta (Dogwood Delights II)

Meatloaf

1 medium onion, chopped
1 tablespoon butter
½ cup stuffing mix
½ cup beef bouillon (broth)
1 pound ground beef
4 sprigs parsley, chopped
3 tablespoons grated Parmesan
   cheese

1 egg, slightly beaten
1 teaspoon salt
¼ teaspoon pepper
Pats of butter
1 (8-ounce) can tomato sauce
1 teaspoon oregano

Sauté onion in butter. In large bowl, mix stuffing and bouillon. Add onion, ground beef, parsley, Parmesan cheese, egg, salt, and pepper; blend. Form into loaf in baking pan. Dot top with butter. Bake 30 minutes in a 375° oven. Combine tomato sauce and oregano. Pour over meatloaf. Bake 20 minutes longer. Serves 4–6.

Reba Bradley, General (Dogwood Delights II)

Colorado Chili Meatloaf

1 sweet red bell pepper,
  chopped
1 small jalapeño pepper,
  chopped
1 (24-ounce) can Italian
  tomatoes, chopped
1 large onion, chopped
1 clove garlic, chopped
¼ cup olive oil

1 pound hamburger meat
½ pound sausage
1 teaspoon oregano
1 teaspoon cumin
1 tablespoon chili powder
1 cup corn
1 cup bread crumbs
1 green onion, chopped
1 cup shredded Cheddar cheese

Sauté peppers, tomatoes, onion, and garlic in oil for 8 minutes, till soft. Mix meats with sautéed vegetables. Add seasonings, corn, bread crumbs, and green onion. Form meatloaf and place in meatloaf pan. Bake at 350° for 1 hour. Sprinkle with shredded cheese and cook 4 more minutes.

Brownie Scott, Marietta, GA (Great Southern Recipes)

Ground Beef Casserole

1 pound ground beef
1 medium onion, chopped
1 bell pepper, chopped
Salt and pepper to taste
2 tablespoons butter

1 (16-ounce) can pork and beans
½ cup ketchup
1 tablespoon Worcestershire
1 tablespoon brown sugar or
  dark syrup

In skillet, sauté beef, onion, bell pepper, salt and pepper in butter. Combine remaining ingredients and mix with beef mixture. Place in shallow baking dish and bake 45 minutes at 375°.

Joyce Gilmore, Savannah, GA (Dogwood Delights)

Onion-Beef Casserole

1½ pounds ground beef
1 envelope onion soup mix
1 teaspoon flour
1 (8-ounce) can tomato sauce

2 cups water
1 cup macaroni, cooked
1 cup grated Cheddar cheese

Brown meat; stir in soup mix, flour, tomato sauce, and water. Simmer 5 minutes. Stir in macaroni; turn into casserole. Sprinkle with cheese. Bake at 400° for 15 minutes.

Pam Burnett, Brookwood-Downtown (Dogwood Delights)

Stuffed Cabbage Rolls

1 pound ground beef
⅓ cup uncooked regular rice
1 egg, beaten
2 tablespoons minced onion
1 teaspoon instant onion soup
   mix
2½ teaspoons salt, divided
¼ teaspoon pepper, divided
6–10 large cabbage leaves

1 medium onion, sliced thin
2 tablespoons margarine
1 (10¾-ounce) can tomato soup
1¼ cups water
½ teaspoon chopped celery
½ teaspoon dried parsley
3 tablespoons lemon juice
1 teaspoon sugar

Combine beef, rice, egg, minced onion, onion soup mix, 1½ teaspoons salt, and ⅛ teaspoon pepper; mix well. Cook cabbage leaves in boiling salted water 5–7 minutes till just tender; drain. Put equal portions of meat mixture in center of each leaf; fold ends over and fasten with toothpicks. Sauté onion slices in margarine in large skillet till tender. Do not brown. Add tomato soup and remaining ingredients. Stir well. Simmer 10 minutes. Place cabbage rolls in tomato mixture; cover and simmer 1½–2 hours.

Tony Kubiak, General (Dogwood Delights II)

Sloppy Joes

1 pound lean ground beef	Salt and pepper to taste
1 small onion, chopped	1½ cups stewed tomatoes
½ green bell pepper, chopped	3 ounces tomato paste
1 cup chopped celery	3 tablespoons barbeque sauce

Brown beef; add onion, pepper, celery, salt and pepper. Add remaining ingredients and simmer ½ hour. Good on cheese buns. Serves 6.

Beverly Brodie, Area (Dogwood Delights II)

Beef Tips and Noodles

1 (10¾-ounce) can cream of mushroom soup	1 cup water
1 envelope onion soup mix	1 pound sirloin tips
1 (4-ounce) can mushrooms, drained	1 (16-ounce) package wide egg noodles

Preheat oven to 400°. In 9x13-inch baking dish, combine mushroom and onion soups, mushrooms, and water. Mix thoroughly and add beef tips. Turn to coat well. Bake in preheated oven for 1 hour.

While beef tips are cooking, bring a large pot of lightly salted water to a boil. Add pasta and cook 8–10 minutes, or till al dente; drain. Serve beef tips and sauce over noodles.

Howard Peery, Alpharetta, GA (Great Southern Recipes)

Stuffed Pepper Cups

6 medium bell peppers
1 pound ground beef
⅓ cup chopped onion
½ teaspoon salt
Dash of pepper
1 (16-ounce) can tomatoes

½ cup water
½ cup uncooked long-grain
  rice
1 teaspoon Worcestershire
4 ounces sharp American cheese,
  shredded

Cut off tops of peppers; remove seeds and membrane. Precook in boiling salted water about 5 minutes; drain. Sprinkle inside of cups generously with salt.

Cook ground beef and onion till meat is lightly browned; season with salt and pepper. Add tomatoes, water, rice, and Worcestershire. Cover and simmer till rice is tender, about 15 minutes. Stir in cheese. Stuff prepared peppers and stand upright in baking dish. Bake uncovered at 350° for 20–25 minutes.

Sharon Wright, Jonesboro-South Fulton (Dogwood Delights)

Emma M. Nutt was the first female employee for the Bell Telephone Company. She was hired at the Boston exchange September 1, 1878, and continued until her retirement in 1915. Her 37 years as an operator began a tradition of long service.

Cranberry Glazed Meatballs

2 pounds ground round
1 cup cornflakes or herb
 stuffing
⅓ cup parsley flakes

2 eggs
2 tablespoons soy sauce
¼ teaspoon garlic powder
2 tablespoons minced onion

Combine all ingredients and shape into 60 balls.

GLAZE:
1 (16-ounce) can jellied
 cranberry sauce
2 tablespoons dark brown
 sugar

1 tablespoon bottled lemon juice
1 (12-ounce) can chili sauce

Combine all ingredients and cook over moderate heat till smooth. Pour over meatballs and bake, uncovered, 30 minutes at 350°.

Jane Pelham-Doyle, Area (Dogwood Delights II)

Quick Italian Skillet

1 medium green bell pepper,
 sliced
2 teaspoons oil
12 ounces ground beef
1 envelope Italian salad
 dressing mix

1 (14½-ounce) can chopped
 tomatoes
1 (4-ounce) can sliced
 mushrooms

Sauté green pepper in oil in skillet till tender. Remove with slotted spoon. Add ground beef. Cook till brown and crumbly, stirring constantly; drain. Sprinkle with salad dressing mix. Add tomatoes, mushrooms, and green pepper; mix well. Simmer 5–10 minutes, or till heated through. Serve over rice or pasta. Yields 4 servings.

Janet M. Rowland, Athens-Gainesville Council
(Lawfully Good Eating)

Mock Beef Stroganoff

1 (10¾-ounce) can cream of
onion soup
1 (10¾-ounce) can cream of
celery soup
1 (10¾-ounce) can cream of
mushroom soup

1 pound stew beef cubes (chuck)
1 (6-ounce) can sliced
mushrooms
Extra wide egg noodles

Mix soups together in casserole dish. Put meat and mushrooms in
and stir. Bake uncovered at 350° for 2½–3 hours till meat is tender.
Stir occasionally. Cook noodles according to package directions.
Add cooked noodles to meat mixture and stir. Serves 8.

Denni Coker, General (Dogwood Delights)

SOS

2 (4-ounce) jars dried beef
½ green bell pepper, chopped
1 small onion, chopped
1 tablespoon butter
1 (10¾-ounce) can cream of
mushroom soup

1 soup can milk
3 boiled eggs, chopped
Mushrooms (optional)
Pimentos (optional)

In saucepan, boil dried beef about 5 minutes; drain and cool. Sauté
pepper and onion in butter till soft. In large saucepan, mix soup
and milk till smooth. Break beef into small pieces and add to soup
mixture. Add remaining ingredients; simmer about 30 minutes.
Serve over fried eggs or toast. Serves 5–6.

Jerry D. Witt, General (Dogwood Delights)

Old-Fashioned Pot Roast

1 (3-pound) boneless beef
  chuck roast
6 tablespoons all-purpose
  flour, divided
6 tablespoons butter, divided
3 cups hot water

2 teaspoons beef bouillon
1 medium onion, quartered
1 celery rib, cut into pieces
1 teaspoon salt
½ teaspoon pepper
4 carrots, cut into 2-inch pieces

Sprinkle roast with 1 tablespoon flour. In a Dutch oven, brown roast on all sides in half the butter. Add water, bouillon, onion, celery, salt, and pepper; bring to a boil. Reduce heat; cover and simmer 1 hour. Add carrots; cover and simmer 45–60 minutes longer or till meat is tender. Remove meat and carrots to serving platter and keep warm. Strain cooking juices; set aside.

In the same Dutch oven, melt remaining butter. Stir in remaining flour; cook and stir till bubbly. Add 2 cups cooking juices and blend till smooth. Cook and stir till thickened; add additional cooking juices till gravy reaches desired consistency. Yields 6–8 servings.

Teresa L. Roberts, Conyers, GA (Great Southern Recipes)

Pot Roast and Gravy

2 tablespoons oil
Flour
1 beef roast
2 cups water
1 (16-ounce) can V8 juice
1 onion, cut in chunks
Dash of Worcestershire
A-1 Steak Sauce
Heinz 57 Sauce
1 pound baby carrots
5 potatoes, peeled, cut into
 chunks
4 tablespoons cornstarch

Heat oil in Dutch oven. Rub flour on both sides of roast and sear in oil. Add water, V8 juice, onion, and Worcestershire. Cover top of roast with A-1 and Heinz 57 Sauce. Add water to about ⅔ up side of roast. Bring to a boil and simmer, covered, till roast is cooked to right temperature, at least 1 hour. Add carrots to pot and simmer 20 minutes. Add potatoes and cook till potatoes are done.

Remove roast, carrots, and potatoes from pot. Mix cornstarch with enough water to make thick liquid. Heat gravy to a boil and add cornstarch mixture to thicken, stirring well.

Susan Sloan, Fayetteville, GA (Great Southern Recipes)

Slow-Cooker Pot Roast

1 medium beef roast
1 envelope onion soup mix
1 (10¾-ounce) can cream of
 chicken soup
5–6 carrots, peeled, cut
5–6 potatoes, peeled, cut

Preheat slow cooker on HIGH. Place roast in slow cooker; sprinkle with soup mix. Spread with soup; do not add water. Cook on HIGH 30 minutes; reduce heat to LOW. Add carrots and potatoes. Cook till done to taste (5 hours or longer). Yields 5–6 servings.

Sue C. Seitz, Athens-Gainesville Council (Lawfully Good Eating)

London Broil

1 (2- to 2½-pound) round steak
1 teaspoon unseasoned meat
  tenderizer
1 tablespoon sugar
2 tablespoons soy sauce
1 teaspoon salt
1 teaspoon Ac'cent
2 tablespoons dry sherry
1 tablespoon honey
Sliced mushrooms

Pierce steak with sharp fork. Combine remaining ingredients except mushrooms and pour over steak; let stand at room temperature 1 hour, turning once. Broil with surface of meat about 3 inches below heat. Allow 5 minutes cooking time for top side, approximately 3 minutes for lower. Add mushrooms to drippings and serve as a sauce.

Mary Glen Stevens, General (Dogwood Delights)

Crockpot Bar-B-Que

2 pounds lean beef or pork,
  cut into bite-size pieces
2 medium onions, chopped
1 green bell pepper, chopped
1 (6-ounce) can tomato paste
3 tablespoons vinegar
3 tablespoons Worcestershire
1 stalk celery, chopped
3 cloves garlic, pressed
1½ teaspoons Tabasco

Brown meat and onions. Stir in remaining ingredients. Simmer in crockpot on LOW for at least 5 hours or till meat strings apart. Yields 15 sandwiches.

Karen Hartley, General (Dogwood Delights)

Apricot Ribs

1 (17-ounce) can apricot halves
⅓ cup packed brown sugar
3 tablespoons vinegar
1 clove garlic, minced

4 teaspoons soy sauce
⅛ teaspoon ground ginger
6 pounds pork ribs, cut into 2-rib portions

Drain apricots, reserving ⅓ cup syrup. Purée in blender with reserved syrup. Combine with brown sugar, vinegar, garlic, soy sauce, and ginger in saucepan. Simmer over medium heat 10–15 minutes, stirring occasionally. Grill ribs over medium-hot coals 50 minutes, basting with apricot sauce during last 30 minutes. Yields 6 servings.

Linda Kite, Macon Council (Lawfully Good Eating)

Orange Glazed Country-Style Ribs

⅓ cup orange marmalade
¼ cup lemon juice
¼ cup soy sauce
1 clove garlic, minced

2 teaspoons cornstarch
2 tablespoons water
5 pounds country-style pork ribs

In saucepan, mix marmalade, lemon juice, soy sauce, and garlic. Mix cornstarch and water till smooth. Stir into saucepan. Cook, stirring constantly, just till mixture thickens and boils.

Place ribs in large pan. Add enough water to cover; heat to boiling. Reduce heat and cook till pretty much done. Remove ribs and drain.

Place on grill 3 inches from medium coals; baste with orange sauce. Cook about 30 minutes, turning frequently while basting with orange sauce. Allow glaze to caramelize on ribs. Makes about 4 servings.

Howard Peery, Alpharetta, GA (Great Southern Recipes)

Marinated Pork Tenderloin

¼ cup soy sauce
2 tablespoons dry red wine
1 tablespoon honey
1 tablespoon brown sugar

1 clove garlic, minced
½ teaspoon cinnamon
1 green onion, minced
2 lean pork tenderloins

Combine soy sauce, wine, honey, brown sugar, garlic, cinnamon, and green onion in airtight container; mix well. Add pork tenderloins. Marinate in refrigerator 2 hours to overnight. Remove tenderloins, tying together, if necessary; reserve marinade. Grill over medium-hot coals 40–60 minutes, basting every 15 minutes with reserved marinade. May also bake in 375° oven 40 minutes. Slice into thin strips to serve. Yields 6–8 servings.

Lorrie Bolton, Athens-Gainesville Council
(Lawfully Good Eating)

Crockpot Orange Pork Roast

1 (3- to 4-pound) pork roast
½ teaspoon salt
¼ teaspoon pepper
1 (6-ounce) can frozen orange
   juice, thawed

¼ cup brown sugar
⅛ teaspoon ground nutmeg
⅛ teaspoon ground allspice

Place roast in crockpot; sprinkle with salt and pepper. Combine juice, brown sugar, and spices; pour over roast. Cover and cook on HIGH 1 hour. Reduce heat to LOW and cook 8 hours.

Before serving, skim juices and pour liquid into a small pan. Whisk flour and water into mixture; bring to a boil, stirring till thickened. Serve with roast. Yields 6 servings.

Doris Thompson, Grayson, GA (Great Southern Recipes)

Pork Chops à la Mushroom

4–6 center-cut pork chops
½ teaspoon salt
¼ teaspoon pepper
½ teaspoon garlic salt
½ teaspoon lemon pepper
2 tablespoons oil

1 tablespoon Worcestershire
¼ pound sliced fresh
  mushrooms
1 (10¾-ounce) can cream of
  mushroom soup
½ cup sour cream

Season pork chops with salt, pepper, garlic salt, and lemon pepper. Brown chops in oil in large skillet over medium heat 15–20 minutes. Add Worcestershire and mushrooms; simmer till mushrooms are tender. Combine soup and sour cream. Pour over pork chops. Cover and simmer 30 minutes longer. Serve with rice. Makes 4–6 servings.

Denise Love, Austell-Marietta (Dogwood Delights II)

Pork Chop 'n Potato Bake

6 pork chops
Oil
Seasoned salt
1 (10¾-ounce) can condensed
  cream of celery soup
½ cup milk
½ cup sour cream

¼ teaspoon black pepper
1 (24-ounce) package frozen hash
  brown potatoes, thawed
1 cup shredded Cheddar cheese,
  divided
1 (3-ounce) can French fried
  onions, divided

Brown pork chops in oil in skillet. Sprinkle with seasoned salt; set aside. Combine soup, milk, sour cream, pepper, and ½ teaspoon seasoned salt. Stir in potatoes, ½ cup cheese, and ½ can French fried onions. Spoon mixture into 9x13-inch baking dish. Arrange pork chops over potatoes. Bake, covered, at 350° for 40 minutes. Top with remaining cheese and onions. Bake, uncovered, 5 minutes longer. Serves 6.

Kathy Edwards, Chamblee-North Fulton (Dogwood Delights II)

Pork Chop Casserole

1 (7-ounce) box Minute Rice
½ envelope dry onion soup
  mix
1 (10¾-ounce) can cream of
  mushroom soup

1¼ cups boiling water
¼ cup rose wine
4 or more pork chops

Combine rice, soup mix, mushroom soup, water, and wine in a large buttered casserole. Brown pork chops and place on top of rice mixture. Bake covered for 1 hour and 15 minutes at 375°. Serves 3–4.

Jamie Langston, Chamblee-North Fulton (Dogwood Delights)

Hawaiian Ham

1 (3- to 4-pound) boneless
  precooked ham
1 (15-ounce) can sliced
  pineapple, drained, reserve
  syrup
3 tablespoons butter

3 tablespoons all-purpose flour
2 tablespoons tomato sauce
⅓ cup brown sugar
⅓ cup vinegar
3 tablespoons prepared mustard

Have ham sliced into ½-inch-thick slices. Alternate ham and pineapple slices in large shallow casserole. Melt butter in pan; blend in flour till smooth. Combine reserved pineapple syrup, tomato sauce, brown sugar, vinegar, and mustard; gradually blend into flour mixture. Cook, stirring, till slightly thickened. Pour sauce over ham and pineapple. Bake at 350° for 1 hour. Baste often. Serves 12.

Beverly Brodie, Area (Dogwood Delights II)

Poultry

1954
"500" Series

With the invention of the transistor in 1947, the vacuum tube transmitter was soon replaced. Equipment size was reduced and reliability increased, making telephone service more affordable. The telephone started to become a decorative household item in the early 1950s. Although some colored telephones were available much earlier, they did not gain widespread popularity until the advent of the "500" color series. Besides black, the five basic colors available were white, beige, green, pink, and blue. Standard with all the sets was an adjustable volume control for the bell. An improved, more flexible neoprene jacketed telephone cord replaced the cotton covered cords used since telephony began. As many households began using more than one phone, the telephone returned to the wall in a companion piece to the "500" desk set. The wall set was most often used in the kitchen where counter and table space was at a premium.

Chicken Pot Pie

2–3 cups cut-up cooked
  chicken
1 onion, chopped
4 boiled eggs, chopped
1 (15-ounce) can green beans,
  drained
1 (8-ounce) can corn, drained
1 (8-ounce) can peas, drained
1 (10¾-ounce) can cream of
  mushroom soup
2 (10¾-ounce) cans cream of
  chicken soup
½ cup chicken broth

Layer chicken, onion, and eggs in 9x13-inch casserole dish. Mix remaining ingredients and spread over chicken.

CRUST:
1½ cups milk
1½ sticks margarine, melted
1½ cups self-rising flour

Combine ingredients and spread over chicken and vegetables. Bake for 1½ hours at 350°, or till crust is brown.

Linda Payne, Area (Dogwood Delights II)

Chicken Pot Pie

4 large chicken breasts, cooked
1 (16-ounce) bag frozen mixed
  vegetables
1 (10¾-ounce) can cream of
  chicken soup
2 cups chicken broth
Salt and pepper to taste
¾ cup butter, melted
1½ cups milk
1½ cups self-rising flour

Cut up chicken and place in 2-quart casserole dish. Layer frozen vegetables over cut-up chicken. Mix soup and broth and pour over frozen vegetables. Season to taste.

Mix butter, milk, and flour well; pour over chicken mixture. Do not stir. Bake at 350° for 1 hour or till crust rises and browns.

Martha Feagins, Conyers, GA (Great Southern Recipes)

Chicken Ritz

4 chicken breasts, boiled
1 (10¾-ounce) can cream of
  chicken soup
1 (8-ounce) carton sour cream

1 pack Ritz crackers, coarsely
  crushed
¾ stick butter, melted

Remove chicken meat from bones; place on bottom of baking dish. Mix soup and sour cream and spoon on top of chicken. Layer crackers on top. Drizzle melted butter over crackers. Bake at 350° for 35 minutes.

Marjorie Baker, General (Dogwood Delights)

Chicken Casserole

8–10 chicken breast halves
1 (10¾-ounce) can cream of
  celery soup
1 (10¾-ounce) can cream of
  chicken soup

1 soup can milk
1 package Pepperidge Farm
  Stuffing Mix with Herbs
1½ cups chicken broth from
  cooked chicken breasts

Boil chicken breasts and save 1½ cups broth. Dice chicken and put in bottom of casserole dish. Mix the 2 soups and milk together and pour over chicken. Sprinkle stuffing mix over top. Pour broth over stuffing. Place covered dish in 350° oven for 45 minutes. Uncover and cook another 10 minutes.

Jerry Farkas, Marietta, GA (Great Southern Recipes)

Deb's Chicken Casserole

4 chicken breasts
1 cup uncooked rice
1 (10-ounce) package frozen
  broccoli
1–2 (10¾-ounce) cans chicken
  or mushroom soup

½ cup milk
1 cup grated Cheddar cheese,
  divided
½ cup bacon bits

Boil chicken 10 minutes; cool, debone, and cut into chunks. Cook rice according to package instructions; thaw broccoli. Mix soup and milk till smooth; add ⅔ cup cheese, bacon bits, chicken, and broccoli. Mix with rice in lightly greased 2-quart baking dish. Sprinkle with remaining cheese. Bake at 400° for 30 minutes.

Deborah Brooks, General (Dogwood Delights)

Chicken Casserole

2 cups diced cooked chicken or
  turkey
1 (10¾-ounce) can cream of
  chicken soup
1 cup milk
1 cup diced celery
2 teaspoons diced onion

1 cup slivered almonds
½ teaspoon salt
½ teaspoon pepper
1 teaspoon lemon juice
½ cup mayonnaise
2 or 3 hard-boiled eggs, sliced
½ cup cracker crumbs

Combine all ingredients in greased casserole dish. Bake at 425° for 20 minutes.

Jean Hundley, Austell-Marietta (Dogwood Delights II)

Chicken-Yellow Rice Casserole

1 package yellow rice
1 chicken, cooked, deboned, reserve broth
1 (8-ounce) can LeSueur peas

1 stick butter, melted
½ cup grated Cheddar cheese (optional)

Cook rice in broth from chicken. When rice is done, mix all ingredients together except cheese. Place in lightly greased casserole dish. Top with cheese and bake at 350° for 30 minutes.

Shirley Nobles, Decatur-Tucker (Dogwood Delights II)

Chicken Supreme

2½ pounds chicken breasts
1 stalk celery, cut up
½ green bell pepper, chopped
2 (10¾-ounce) cans cream of mushroom soup
1 (10¾-ounce) can cream of celery soup

1 (7-ounce) jar pimentos
1 teaspoon Worcestershire
8–12 ounces thin spaghetti, cooked
Salt and pepper to taste
1 cup shredded sharp Cheddar cheese

Rinse chicken well. Cook with celery in water to cover in saucepan till tender. Drain, reserving stock. Chop chicken into bite-size pieces. Cook green pepper in small amount of reserved chicken stock in saucepan till tender-crisp. Combine chicken, green pepper, soups, pimento, Worcestershire, spaghetti, salt and pepper; mix well. Spoon into lightly greased baking dish. Bake at 350° for 45 minutes. Top with cheese; bake for 15 minutes longer. Yields 8 servings.

Linda Helms, Macon Council (Lawfully Good Eating)

Chicken Dianne

4 large or 8 small chicken
  breast fillets
Pepper to taste
2 tablespoons safflower oil
2 tablespoons margarine
3 tablespoons chopped green
  onions

3 tablespoons chopped parsley
Juice of ½ lemon
3 tablespoons Dijon mustard
½ cup chicken broth

Rinse chicken and pat dry; pound flat between plastic wrap. Sprinkle both sides with pepper. Brown in oil and margarine in skillet over high heat 4 minutes on each side. Remove to warm platter. Add green onions, parsley, and lemon juice to skillet. Sauté 30–60 seconds. Whisk in mustard. Cook 15 seconds. Whisk in chicken broth; cook till smooth. Spoon over chicken. Serve with no-egg yolk noodles, steamed broccoli, or green salad. Yields 4 servings.

Judy Moody, Augusta Council (Lawfully Good Eating)

Detroit, Michigan, was the first city in the nation to assign individual telephone numbers in 1879.

Chicken Enchilada Casserole

4–6 boneless, skinless chicken
  breasts
2 (10-ounce) cans enchilada
  sauce
2 (10¾-ounce) cans cream of
  mushroom soup
2 (10¾-ounce) cans tomato
  soup
Corn tortillas
1 onion, chopped
Shredded cheese

Bake chicken breasts; let cool, then shred. Mix together in a large bowl the enchilada sauce, mushroom soup, and tomato soup. Put some sauce in bottom of a 9x13-inch baking dish. Put a layer of corn tortillas on bottom, then a layer of chicken, then chopped onion, shredded cheese, and sauce mixture; repeat, finishing with sauce on top. Bake at 350° for 30 minutes, and then put a layer of cheese on top. Heat a few more minutes for cheese to melt.

Linda Clabaugh, Blue Ridge, GA (Great Southern Recipes)

Chicken Cordon Bleu Casserole

2 pounds skinless chicken
  breasts, cut into chunks
1 egg, mixed with ½ cup milk
½ cup bread crumbs
8 ounces Swiss cheese, cubed
8 ounces ham, diced
1 (10¾-ounce) can cream of
  chicken soup
1 cup milk

Dip chunks of chicken in egg and milk mixture, then in bread crumbs, coating well. Brown in a little oil in skillet till golden, then place chunks in baking dish. Add cubes of Swiss cheese and small pieces of ham. Combine soup and milk; mix well. Pour over all. Bake about 30 minutes at 350°, or till tender and bubbly. Serves 6.

Sherry Scott, Marietta, GA (Great Southern Recipes)

Easy Chicken Curry

1 cup mayonnaise
1 (10¾-ounce) can cream of
    mushroom soup
1 tablespoon curry powder

2 chicken breasts, broiled
1 bunch fresh broccoli spears,
    steamed
Slivered almonds, toasted

Combine mayonnaise, soup, and curry. Place chicken in flat baking dish. Lay broccoli spears across chicken; cover with sauce. Bake 45 minutes at 350°. Top with almonds and serve.

Hazel Coile, Area (Dogwood Delights)

Chicken and Dumplings

1 chicken, cut up
2 teaspoons salt, divided
4 quarts water
3 stalks celery, chopped

2 cups all-purpose flour
⅓ cup shortening
Water

Place chicken, 1 teaspoon salt, and water in large pot. Bring to a boil, reduce heat, and simmer several hours. During last 30 minutes, add celery. Remove chicken from broth; cool; remove skin and bones. Cut chicken into small chunks.

Sift flour and remaining 1 teaspoon salt together. Cut in shortening and add enough water to make stiff dough. Divide dough in half and place on well-floured wax paper. Roll out very thin. Cut into strips about 1 inch wide and 4 inches long. Sift additional flour on top of strips. Add to boiling broth, one at a time. Working as quickly as possible, repeat procedure with remaining dough. Continue to boil 10 minutes, stirring gently every few minutes to prevent sticking. Add chicken and reheat.

Mary M. Rogera, W. E.-Service/Installation (Dogwood Delights)

Creamed Chicken and Biscuits

½ large onion, chopped
1½ teaspoons butter
4 cups chopped cooked chicken
1 (10¾-ounce) can cream of
  chicken soup
1 (8-ounce) carton sour cream
½ cup milk
½ cup chopped pimentos
1 cup shredded mild Cheddar
  cheese, divided
6 frozen biscuits, thawed

Preheat oven to 350°. Grease bottom and side of 7x11-inch baking dish. Sauté onion in butter till tender. Combine onion, chicken, soup, sour cream, milk, and pimentos in medium bowl; mix well. Spoon mixture into prepared baking dish. Bake 15 minutes. Remove from oven.

Sprinkle baked layer with ¾ cup cheese. Arrange biscuits in single layer over top. Sprinkle with remaining cheese. Bake till biscuits are golden brown and sauce is bubbly, about 25–30 minutes. Serve immediately.

Brenda Harris, Loganville, GA (Great Southern Recipes)

Ma's Chicken Provolone

4 chicken breasts
4 slices ham
2 tablespoons butter
2 tablespoons olive oil
1 cup white wine
4 slices provolone cheese

Rinse and dry chicken. Place between pieces of wax paper. Pound to ¼-inch thickness. Place ham over chicken and roll up. Secure with toothpicks. Heat butter and olive oil in skillet over medium heat. Cook chicken 5–7 minutes per side. Pour wine over chicken. Simmer till reduced by half. Top with slice of cheese on each chicken breast. Simmer till melted. Serve immediately.

Carrie M. Lampkin, Conyers, GA (Great Southern Recipes)

Easy Chicken and Dressing

1 (8-ounce) package cornbread
  stuffing mix
1 stick butter, melted
3–3½ pounds chicken, boiled,
  cut into bite-size pieces
  (reserve broth)

2 (10¾-ounce) cans cream of
  chicken soup

Mix stuffing mix and butter; reserve 1 cup of mixture. Place remaining mixture in 9x13-inch baking dish; top with chicken. Pour soup over chicken; add 2 soup cans broth over this. Poke holes to let it soak in. Top with reserved stuffing mixture. Bake at 350° for 30 minutes.

LeAnne Wilkes, Chamblee-North Fulton (Dogwood Delights II)

Crazy Chicken

6 small chicken breasts
¾ cup apple jelly
¾ teaspoon dry mustard
¾ teaspoon salt

⅛ teaspoon pepper
1 (12-ounce) can Dr Pepper or
  cherry cola

Rinse chicken; pat dry. Place in 10-inch skillet. Combine jelly, dry mustard, salt, and pepper; mix well. Stir in 1 cup Dr Pepper gradually. Pour over chicken. Bring to a boil over high heat; reduce heat to medium-high. Simmer, covered, 10 minutes, basting occasionally. Reduce heat to medium. Simmer, covered, 15 minutes, or till tender, turning and basting several times and adding remaining Dr Pepper, if needed for desired consistency. Spoon sauce over chicken to serve. Serve with rice pilaf, Chinese pea pods, and fruit salad. Yields 6 servings.

Kim Edwards, Athens-Gainesville Council
(Lawfully Good Eating)

Baked Chicken Breast Supreme

6 (12-ounce) chicken breasts
2 cups sour cream
¼ cup lemon juice
4 teaspoons Worcestershire
4 teaspoons celery salt
2 teaspoons paprika
4 cloves garlic, finely chopped

4 teaspoons salt
½ teaspoon pepper
1¾ cups packaged dry bread
    crumbs
½ cup butter
½ cup shortening

Cut chicken breasts in halves; wipe well with damp paper towels. In large bowl, combine sour cream with lemon juice, Worcestershire, celery salt, paprika, garlic, salt, and pepper. Add chicken to sour cream mixture, coating each piece well. Let stand, covered, in refrigerator overnight.

Next day, preheat oven to 350°. Remove chicken from sour cream mixture. Roll in crumbs, coating evenly. Arrange in single layer in large, shallow baking pan. Melt butter and shortening in small saucepan. Spoon half over chicken. Bake chicken, uncovered, 45 minutes. Spoon rest of butter mixture over chicken. Bake 10–15 minutes longer, or till chicken is tender and nicely browned.

Janice Davis, Austell-Marietta (Dogwood Delights II)

The coin-operated pay telephone was patented by William Gray of Hartford, Connecticut, in 1889.

Georgia County Captain

½ cup oil
2 cloves garlic, halved
2 medium onions, thinly sliced
½ cup all-purpose flour
3 teaspoons salt, divided
¼ teaspoon pepper
1 (3½-pound) fryer, cut up
1 teaspoon curry powder
½ cup chopped celery with
leaves

1 green bell pepper, coarsely
chopped
1 (27-ounce) can tomatoes (3½
cups)
1 cup raw rice
¼ cup raisins
2 tablespoons butter
⅓ cup almonds
Snipped parsley

In hot oil, over medium heat, sauté garlic and onions till tender, but not brown; remove from oil.

Meanwhile, combine flour, 1 teaspoon salt, and pepper in paper bag. Coat chicken and brown in oil. Now, add garlic, onions, 2 teaspoons salt, curry powder, celery, pepper, and tomatoes. Cover and simmer 45 minutes till chicken is tender.

Cook rice; add raisins and toss; add butter. In skillet, brown almonds. When chicken is done, arrange rice over chicken and sauce. Sprinkle with almonds and parsley. Makes 4 servings.

Brenda Plunkett, General (Dogwood Delights II)

Chicken Lasagna

5 cups chopped cooked chicken
2 cups chicken broth
1 (10¾-ounce) can cream of
  mushroom soup
1 (8-ounce) can sliced
  mushrooms
1 (7-ounce) can sliced water
  chestnuts
1 (5-ounce) can evaporated milk
Poultry seasoning, salt, and
  pepper to taste
8 lasagna noodles, cooked
¾ cup shredded Cheddar
  cheese

Combine chicken, broth, soup, mushrooms, water chestnuts, evaporated milk, poultry seasoning, salt and pepper in saucepan; mix well. Cook over low heat 10 minutes, stirring to mix well. Alternate layers of chicken mixture, noodles, and cheese in baking dish till all ingredients are used, ending with cheese. Bake at 350° for 45 minutes. Yields 8 servings.

Debbi Palmer, Macon Council (Lawfully Good Eating)

Baked Chicken Breasts

1 (4-ounce) jar dried beef
8 chicken breasts, skinned,
  deboned
8 slices bacon, halved
1 (8-ounce) carton sour cream
1 (10¾-ounce) can cream of
  mushroom soup
½ cup water
Cooked rice or noodles

Soak dried beef in boiling water 2–3 minutes. Chop beef and place in bottom of 9x13-inch baking dish. Wrap each piece of chicken with 2 slices of bacon, and place on top of dried beef. Combine sour cream, soup, and water; pour over chicken. Bake 2 hours at 250°. Serve over hot rice or noodles.

Jamie Langston, Chamblee-North Fulton (Dogwood Delights)

Southern Poppy Seed Chicken

2 cups cooked, chopped
  chicken breasts
1 (10¾-ounce) can cream of
  chicken soup

1 cup sour cream
1 stick butter, melted
1 roll Ritz Crackers, crushed
1 tablespoon poppy seeds

Place chicken in greased 1½-quart shallow baking dish. Blend soup and sour cream and spread over chicken. Combine melted butter, cracker crumbs, and poppy seeds. Spread over chicken. Bake at 350° for 30 minutes.

Janeen B. Aylor, Blairsville, GA (Great Southern Recipes)

Mexican Lasagna

2 (10-ounce) cans chicken
  breasts, drained
2 cups spaghetti sauce
1½ cups picante sauce, divided
1 teaspoon chili powder

8 (6-inch) flour tortillas
2 cups grated Cheddar cheese,
  divided
1 (4-ounce) can diced black
  olives

Place chicken, spaghetti sauce, 1 cup picante sauce, and chili powder in saucepan and simmer 10 minutes.

In casserole dish, spread ½ cup picante sauce on bottom. Place 4 tortillas across the casserole dish. Spread ½ the chicken mixture on top of tortillas. Sprinkle 1 cup cheese on top of mixture. Place remaining tortillas next, then chicken sauce, and cheese. Top with black olives. Cook on 350° for 20 minutes. Let casserole stand 5 minutes before slicing.

Nancy Edenfield, Covington, GA (Great Southern Recipes)

Oven Fried Chicken

¼ cup shortening
¼ cup butter
½ cup all-purpose flour
1 teaspoon salt

1 tablespoon paprika
¼ teaspoon pepper
4–6 chicken breasts

Heat oven to 425°. In oven, melt shortening and butter in 9x13-inch baking dish. Mix flour, salt, pepper, and paprika. Coat chicken with flour mixture. Place chicken, breast side down in baking dish. Cook, uncovered, 30 minutes. Turn chicken and cook 30 minutes longer.

Janet Miles, Austell-Marietta (Dogwood Delights II)

Crispy Fried Chicken

1 (3- to 3½-pound) fryer, cut up   Oil
Salt and white pepper

FIRST BATTER:
1 cup tepid water
1 teaspoon salt
½ teaspoon white pepper

1 cup all-purpose flour
2 drops yellow food coloring

SECOND BATTER:
1 cup all-purpose flour
1 teaspoon salt

½ teaspoon white pepper

Rinse chicken pieces under running water. Pat dry. Sprinkle with salt and white pepper; set aside. Fill a 12-inch frying pan or deep-fryer half full with oil. Heat to 325°.

Combine ingredients of First Batter. Place chicken pieces in batter. Combine ingredients of Second Batter. Lift chicken from First Batter and roll in Second Batter. Shake off excess flour. Fry about 8 minutes on each side. Drain well on paper towels. Serves 4.

Pat Gulley, Decatur-Tucker (Dogwood Delights II)

Roasted Stuffed Cornish Hens

1 cup uncooked wild rice
2 cups chicken stock
1 cup finely chopped onion
1 cup finely chopped celery
½ cup margarine
1 (11-ounce) can Mandarin
   oranges
1 cup golden raisins
1 cup finely chopped pecans
½ teaspoon poultry seasoning
½ teaspoon sage

1 teaspoon salt
1 teaspoon pepper
1 chicken bouillon cube
1 cup hot water
6 Cornish game hens
Melted margarine
Additional salt and pepper to
   taste
2 tablespoons all-purpose flour
1–1½ cups water

Cook rice in chicken stock in saucepan 45 minutes or till tender. Sauté onion and celery in margarine in saucepan till tender. Drain oranges, reserving ½ cup juice. Add rice, raisins, Mandarin oranges, pecans, poultry seasoning, sage, and 1 teaspoon salt and pepper to onion mixture; mix well. Dissolve bouillon cube in 1 cup hot water. Add to stuffing mixture; mix well. Rinse hens inside and out, and pat dry. Stuff body and neck cavities with rice mixture. Place in roasting pan sprayed with nonstick cooking spray. Brush with melted margarine; sprinkle with salt and pepper to taste. Roast at 375° for 1–1½ hours, or till tender, basting occasionally with additional chicken stock. Remove hens to warm serving platter. Stir 2 tablespoons flour into drippings. Add reserved Mandarin orange juice and 1–1½ cups water. Simmer till thickened, stirring constantly. Serve sauce with hens. Yields 6 servings.

Patty Steuer, Albany Council (Lawfully Good Eating)

Turkey and Mushroom Meatloaf Patties

3 tablespoons olive oil, divided
6 ounces portobello
  mushrooms, chopped
1 shallot, chopped
1⅓ pounds ground turkey

3 or 4 sprigs fresh sage,
  chopped
1 tablespoon Worcestershire
½ cup bread crumbs
1 egg, beaten

Heat nonstick skillet over medium heat. Add 2 tablespoons olive oil, chopped mushrooms, and shallot; sauté 5–6 minutes. Remove from heat to cool. Add turkey to mushroom mixture. Make a well in center of meat; add sage, Worcestershire, bread crumbs, and beaten egg. Mix well. Form 4 equal oval patties. Add remaining 1 tablespoon olive oil to original skillet. Cook patties 6 minutes on each side over medium heat.

Brenda Borland, Social Circle, GA (Great Southern Recipes)

Turkey Casserole

1 (16-ounce) package frozen,
  chopped broccoli, thawed,
  drained
2½ cups diced cooked turkey
1 (10¾-ounce) can cream of
  mushroom soup

1 (10¾-ounce) can cream of
  chicken soup
2 slices whole-wheat bread,
  toasted, cut in squares
½ cup grated Cheddar cheese

Mix broccoli, turkey, and soups together. In a 2-quart casserole dish, layer turkey mixture, bread squares, more turkey, more bread squares. Top with cheese. Bake 25–30 minutes at 350° or microwave 15–20 minutes on HIGH. Serves 4.

Lori Kelly, General (Dogwood Delights)

Crockpot Dressing

½ cup self-rising cornmeal
1½ cups self-rising flour
1 cup chopped onion
1 cup milk
5 eggs

3 boneless chicken breasts
1 (10¾-ounce) can cream of
  chicken soup
1 stick margarine

Mix together cornmeal, flour, onion, milk, and eggs. Bake in greased pan at 350° for 30 minutes. Cool and crumble bread. Boil chicken breasts; strain broth and chop chicken.

Mix crumbled cornbread, chicken, and soup. Place in crockpot. Cut stick of margarine into pieces and place on top. Cook on HIGH 1 hour or LOW 2 hours. Serves 4–6.

Martha Jung LM, Buford, GA (Great Southern Recipes)

Lemon Barbecue Sauce

1 clove garlic
½ teaspoon salt
¼ cup oil
½ cup fresh lemon juice

2 tablespoons grated onion
½ teaspoon pepper
1 teaspoon Worcestershire

Mash garlic with salt in bowl. Add oil, lemon juice, onion, pepper, and Worcestershire; mix well. Chill 24 hours. Use as a basting sauce for grilling chicken. Yields 1 cup.

Virginia Stembridge, Macon Council (Lawfully Good Eating)

$\mathcal{S}$eafood

1959
Princess

The desk set received a smart, new look. Compactness, attractive styling and illuminated dial (it lights up when you lift the handset or you can keep it on as a night light) contributed to the all-around usefulness of the Princess set. Featured in a variety or colors, including pastels, its design appealed to women and teenage girls. The Princess was unique in two aspects: it required an external electric transformer to power the light-up dial, and when production began it did not contain enough room for a bell ringer, so an external ringer was required. The Princess model remained in production until 1994 with several modifications throughout the years.

With the first transcontinental microwave transmitting system now in operation, true number calling is instituted—that is, seven numerical digits without letters or names—although it took more than fifteen years to implement throughout the system. But cables provide much higher signal quality, avoid atmospheric interference, and offer greater capacity and security.

Bar-B-Cued Shrimp

1 pound butter
1 pound margarine
6 ounces Worcestershire
8 tablespoons finely chopped
  ground black pepper
1 teaspoon ground rosemary

4 lemons, sliced
1 teaspoon Tabasco
4 teaspoons salt
2–4 cloves garlic (optional)
8–10 pounds jumbo shrimp,
  head and shells on

In a saucepan, melt butter and margarine. Add Worcestershire, pepper, rosemary, lemon slices, Tabasco, salt, and garlic; mix thoroughly. Divide shrimp between 2 large, shallow pans and pour heated sauce over each. Stir well. Cook in a 400° oven 15–20 minutes, turning once. Shells should be pink, the meat white and not translucent. Serves about 20 shrimp per person.

Debbie Elliott, W. E.-Region (Dogwood Delights)

Shrimp Scampi

1 pound shrimp, peeled
Butter
¼ cup extra dry vermouth
Creole seasoning to taste

Chopped parsley to taste
½ cup whipping cream
1 teaspoon hollandaise sauce
  mix

Stir-fry shrimp in butter in skillet 3 minutes. Stir in vermouth and Creole seasoning; cook 8 minutes. Remove shrimp to warm platter. Add parsley to skillet. Simmer till pan liquid is reduced. Stir in cream and sauce. Simmer till thickened, stirring constantly. Add shrimp; simmer till heated through. Serve over rice or noodles. Yields 4–6 servings.

Lamar County Sheriff's Department (Lawfully Good Eating)

Shrimp Casserole

1 (8-ounce) package stuffing
  mix, divided
1 stick butter, melted
1 (10¾-ounce) can cream of
  chicken soup

1 pound shrimp, peeled, boiled
1 (8-ounce) carton sour cream
1 small onion, grated

Preheat oven to 325°. Place ½ stuffing mix in bottom of greased 8x8-inch baking dish. Pour melted butter on top. Mix remaining ingredients in bowl. Pour over stuffing mix; top with remaining dry stuffing mix. Bake 25 minutes.

Jean Jiles, Austell-Marietta (Dogwood Delights)

Fried Shrimp–The Very Best

1 pound fresh shrimp
1 (5-ounce) can evaporated milk
2 eggs
1 teaspoon baking powder

1 tablespoon vinegar
Creole seasoning
1 cup all-purpose flour

Remove shells and clean shrimp. Make a mixture of milk, eggs, baking powder, and vinegar. Marinate shrimp in mixture at least 1 hour. Remove; season lightly with Creole seasoning. Dip in flour and fry at 380° not more than 10 minutes. Serves 1–2.

Bill Smith (Great Southern Recipes)

Shrimp Creole

1 medium onion, chopped
3 stalks celery, chopped
1 small green bell pepper, finely chopped
1 stick margarine, divided
1 pound shrimp, peeled, deveined, cut up
¼ cup all-purpose flour
2 (14½-ounce) cans chopped tomatoes
1 teaspoon chili powder
1 teaspoon garlic powder
Salt and pepper to taste
Cooked rice

Cook onion, celery, and pepper till tender in ½ stick margarine in Dutch oven. Cook shrimp in remaining ½ stick margarine till pink. Remove shrimp and brown flour. Add this to onion mixture. Add chopped tomatoes and juices, along with spices and shrimp. Mix well; let simmer about 20 minutes. Serve over rice.

Shirley Clary, Decatur-Tucker (Dogwood Delights II)

Smothered Okra and Shrimp

2 medium onions, chopped
1 green bell pepper, chopped
1 tomato, diced
Parsley flakes
4 pounds okra, fresh or frozen, cut up
1 tablespoon oil
2 pounds shrimp, peeled, deveined
1 (1-pound) package smoked sausage, cut up
Garlic powder
Season-All
Seafood seasoning

Sauté onions, bell pepper, tomato, parsley flakes, and okra in oil about 15 minutes. Add shrimp, sausage, and seasonings to taste. Simmer about 1 hour, or till okra is tender and cooked down.

Rachael Henry-Hood, Jacksonville, FL (Great Southern Recipes)

Shrimp and Onion Casserole

2 pounds cooked peeled
  shrimp
1 medium Vidalia onion,
  chopped
2 cups shredded cheese

1 pound fresh mushrooms
1 (10¾-ounce) can cream of
  chicken soup
1 (3-ounce) can French-fried
  onions

Combine first 5 ingredients in bowl; mix well. Pour into greased baking dish. Bake at 350° for 30 minutes. Sprinkle with French-fried onions. Bake till browned. Serve hot. Yields 6–8 servings.

Ned F. DeLoach, Sheriff, and the Staff of the Tattnall County Sheriff's Department (Lawfully Good Eating)

Seafood Casserole

1 (8-ounce) package cream
  cheese
1 stick plus 2 tablespoons
  butter, divided
1 pound raw shrimp, peeled
1 large onion, chopped
1 green bell pepper, chopped
2 ribs celery, chopped
1 (10¾-ounce) can cream of
  mushroom soup

1½ teaspoons garlic salt
Creole seasoning to taste
1 teaspoon hot pepper sauce
½ teaspoon cayenne pepper
1 pint crabmeat
2 cups cooked rice
1 cup grated Cheddar cheese
4–6 saltine crackers, crushed

In small saucepan, melt cream cheese and 1 stick butter. Set aside. In a large skillet, melt remaining 2 tablespoons butter, and sauté shrimp, onion, bell pepper, and celery. Add cream cheese mixture to shrimp and vegetables, then add soup and seasonings; mix well. Stir in crabmeat and rice. Pour into a greased 9x13-inch baking dish. Top with cheese and crumbs. Bake at 350° for 20–30 minutes till heated thoroughly. Yields 8 servings.

Debbie Goss, Pace, FL (Great Southern Recipes)

Low Country Seafood Boil

8 medium potatoes, quartered
8 large sweet onions, quartered
2 pounds hot country link
   sausage, cooked, with their
   drippings
6 heads garlic, broken into
   cloves
3 hot red peppers, chopped
6 lemons, halved
1 cup cider vinegar

Salt to taste
16 ears fresh corn, cleaned
Tabasco
Freshly ground black pepper
6 pounds raw shrimp, in shells
16 live blue crabs
4 cups cocktail sauce
4 cups butter, melted
2 pounds sour cream

Fill a large pot a little more than half full with water. Place over fire and bring to a boil. Place potatoes and onions in boiling water; bring back to a boil and cook 20 minutes. Add sausage and drippings, garlic, hot peppers, lemons, and vinegar; simmer 15 minutes. Add salt and corn and bring back to a rapid boil. The vegetables should be just done. Taste for seasoning; add Tabasco, pepper, and salt, if needed.

Add shrimp and crabs; this will bring down the heat. Simmer till done, about 15 minutes. Remove potatoes, sausage, corn, crab, and shrimp; heap into a large serving platter. Discard onions, garlic, peppers, and lemons. Serve with cocktail sauce, melted butter, and sour cream. Good for a large group.

Bill Smith (Great Southern Recipes)

Catfish Fillets with Horseradish Sauce

4 scallions or green onions,
  chopped
¼ cup prepared horseradish
⅓ cup dry bread crumbs

¼ cup butter, softened
Salt to taste
4 catfish fillets

Combine scallions, horseradish, bread crumbs, and butter in small bowl; mix well. Sprinkle salt on catfish fillets. Place on buttered broiler pan. Spoon horseradish mixture on top of each fillet, pressing lightly. Broil 6–8 inches from heat source 8 minutes, or till crispy and browned. Serve immediately. Yields 4 servings.

Art and Pauline Davis, Friends of the Pioneers
(Lawfully Good Eating)

Cheesy Broiled Tilapia

2 pounds tilapia fillets
2 tablespoons lemon juice
½ cup grated Parmesan cheese
¼ cup butter, melted

3 tablespoons mayonnaise
¼ teaspoon salt
Dash of hot sauce (optional)

Place fillets in single layer on nonstick 11x15-inch pan. Brush with lemon juice. Combine remaining ingredients; set aside.

Broil fillets 4–6 minutes or till fish flakes with a fork. Remove from oven. Spread with cheese mixture. Broil till golden brown and bubbly.

Betty S. Standard, Covington, GA (Great Southern Recipes)

Tuna Dorito Casserole

1 tablespoon butter
¼ cup chopped onion
1 (10¾-ounce) can cream of
mushroom soup
1 (5-ounce) can evaporated
milk, or ⅔ cup milk
⅓ cup shredded Cheddar
cheese
1 (7-ounce) can tuna, drained

1 (4-ounce) can sliced
mushrooms, drained
½ cup chopped ripe olives
2 teaspoons lemon juice
1 (2-ounce) jar chopped
pimentos, drained
3 cups crushed Doritos
Grated Parmesan cheese
Paprika

Melt butter in saucepan and sauté onion till tender. Add soup, milk, and cheese and heat thoroughly, stirring constantly. Add tuna, mushrooms, olives, lemon juice, and pimentos. In a 2-quart greased casserole dish, place a layer of Doritos, top with ½ tuna mixture; repeat layers till all is used. Top with Parmesan cheese and paprika. Bake at 375° for 20–25 minutes.

Judy Barnett, W.E.-Region (Dogwood Delights)

Tuna Casserole

2 tablespoons margarine,
melted
2 tablespoons flour
1 (5-ounce) can evaporated
milk

1 can water
¾ cup grated cheese
1 (7-ounce) can tuna, drained
2 cups cooked noodles

Blend melted margarine and flour. Add milk and water. Cook over medium heat till thick. Remove from heat. Add cheese, tuna, and noodles. Place in casserole dish and bake at 400° for 30 minutes.

LeAnne Wilkes, Chamblee-North Fulton (Dogwood Delights II)

Seafood au Gratin

SAUCE:

2 cups milk, divided
½ cup grated Cheddar cheese
½ cup Cheez Whiz

½ teaspoon salt
Dash of black pepper
¼ cup all-purpose flour

Mix 1½ cups milk with grated cheese, Cheez Whiz, salt, and pepper in heavy saucepan. Cook, stirring constantly, over medium heat till cheese melts and mixture boils. Mix flour with remaining ½ cup milk till smooth. Stir into cheese mixture till thickened. Simmer 20 minutes.

1 pound crabmeat
1 pound cooked, peeled shrimp

½–2 cups grated Cheddar
cheese

Preheat oven to 350°. Combine crabmeat, shrimp, and Sauce. Pour into casserole dish and top with grated cheese. Bake about 30 minutes, or till bubbly.

Betty Long, Brookwood-Downtown (Dogwood Delights)

In the early days, operators working at a large switchboard would answer an incoming telephone call and connect it manually to the party being called. The first automatic telephone exchange was patented by Almon Strowger of Kansas City in 1891 and installed in 1892, but manual switchboards remained in common use. The last manual switchboard in the Southern Bell region was removed from service in Rosedale, Mississippi, on September 21, 1969.

Pan-Fried Crab Cakes
with Hollandaise and Almonds

1 pound picked crabmeat,
  cooked
1 cup bread crumbs
⅓ cup milk
¼ cup mayonnaise
1 egg, lightly beaten
2 tablespoons finely chopped
  parsley
2 tablespoons finely chopped
  green onions

½ teaspoon baking powder
½ teaspoon salt
¼ teaspoon ground white
  pepper
1 package hollandaise sauce mix
1 small bag sliced almonds
2 tablespoons unsalted butter
2 tablespoons oil
All-purpose flour

Place crabmeat in a large bowl. Cover with bread crumbs and pour milk on top. Combine mayo, egg, parsley, green onions, baking powder, salt, and pepper in separate bowl. Pour over crab mixture and toss till mixed.

Shape into 10 (2½-inch) patties. Place in refrigerator, covered, 1 hour. Prepare Hollandaise according to directions. Toast almonds in 400° oven for 5 minutes; check occasionally.

Heat butter and oil in large skillet over medium heat. Dust crab cakes with flour and fry till golden brown, about 4 minutes on each side. Top with hollandaise and toasted almonds. Serve immediately. Serves 5.

Bill Smith (Great Southern Recipes)

Crab Casserole

¾ cup sweet milk
1 pound crabmeat
1 medium onion, chopped
½ medium green bell pepper, finely chopped
1 (4-ounce) jar pimentos

Black and red pepper to taste
Seafood seasoning to taste
1 tablespoon mayonnaise
Bread crumbs
Sprinkle of Ac'cent
½ cup butter

Pour milk over crabmeat, onion, and green pepper. Mix in pimento and seasonings; add mayonnaise and toss together. Pour into greased casserole dish. Mix bread crumbs with Ac'cent and butter; cover casserole. Preheat oven to 500°, turn back to 375° and bake 30 minutes.

Bernice D. Head, Austell-Marietta; Cece Dixon, Austell-Marietta
(Dogwood Delights II)

Beula's Salmon Patties

1 (16-ounce) can salmon
1 egg
¼ cup mayonnaise
¾ sleeve saltine crackers, crushed

1 medium onion, chopped
Texas Pete hot sauce to taste (optional)

Mix all ingredients. Place in muffin pan, sprayed with Pam. Bake at 350° for 25–30 minutes. Makes 12 patties.

Zaida B. Prado (Great Southern Recipes)

Oyster Casserole

¾ cup butter
2 sleeves saltine crackers,
  crumbled

2 (3-ounce) cans oysters
1 cup milk
Tabasco to taste

Melt butter in saucepan. Add cracker crumbs, stirring well. Spread in baking dish. Drain oysters, reserving liquid. Arrange oysters over cracker mixture. Mix reserved oyster liquid with milk. Pour over oysters. Sprinkle with Tabasco. Bake at 350° for 30 minutes. Yields 4–6 servings.

Mary Beth Higgs, Georgia Sheriff's Youth Homes
(Lawfully Good Eating)

Tartar Sauce

½ cup mayonnaise
¼ teaspoon Worcestershire
½ teaspoon grated onion

1 tablespoon chopped pickles
1 tablespoon chopped olives
1 tablespoon lemon juice

Combine all ingredients; mix well. Store in refrigerator. Yields ¾ cup.

Marie Driver, Athens-Gainesville Council
(Lawfully Good Eating)

Cakes

1964
Touch-Tone

As America neared the 200 million mark in population, a new era in telephoning services began with push-button calling. Touch-Tone service was introduced, limiting errors and increasing the speed of dialing. A keypad replaced the familiar rotary "pulse" dial, and early Touch-Tone sets had only ten buttons. (The * and # keys were added in 1968.) The Touch-Tone system could travel across microwave transmitter links and work rapidly with solid state computer-controlled phone exchanges. A tone is produced as long as a key is depressed. No matter how long you press, the tone is decoded as the appropriate digit. The shortest duration in which a digit can be sent and decoded is about 100 milliseconds by automatic dialers. A twelve-digit long-distance phone number can be dialed by an automatic phone dialer in a little more than a second—about as long as it takes a pulse dial to send a single "0" digit.

Sour Cream Pound Cake

3 sticks butter, softened
3 cups sugar
1 (8-ounce) carton sour cream
6 eggs

1 teaspoon vanilla
3 cups cake flour
⅛ teaspoon baking soda

Cream butter and sugar; add sour cream. Mix well. Add eggs, one at a time, beating after each one. Add vanilla and mix. Sift flour and baking soda; add in ⅓ portions to creamed mixture. Beat batter very well. Bake at 350° for 1 hour and 15 minutes.

Lynda Buice, General (Dogwood Delights II)

Cream Cheese Pound Cake

3 sticks butter or margarine,
   softened
1 (8-ounce) package cream
   cheese, softened
3 cups sugar
3 cups cake flour, sifted before
   measuring, divided

6 eggs
1 teaspoon vanilla flavoring
1 teaspoon coconut flavoring
   (optional)
1 teaspoon pineapple flavoring
   (optional)

Cream butter and cream cheese with sugar. Add 1 cup flour and 2 eggs alternately until all are blended. Add flavoring. Cook in well-greased tube pan at 350° for 1 hour and 45 minutes. This cake needs no baking powder, salt or baking soda. Serves 15–20.

Faye Powers, General; Marvella Garriss, Chamblee-North Fulton (Dogwood Delights); Pam Crawford, Athens-Gainesville Council (Lawfully Good Eating)

Chocolate Pound Cake

3¼ cups all-purpose flour
½ teaspoon salt
½ teaspoon baking powder
½ cup cocoa
1 cup margarine, softened

½ cup shortening
3 cups sugar
2 teaspoons vanilla
5 eggs
1 cup milk

Heat oven to 325°. Grease and flour a 10-inch tube pan. Stir flour, salt, baking powder, and cocoa together; set aside. Cream margarine, shortening, and sugar together till colored and fluffy. Add vanilla. Beat in eggs, one at a time. Add flour mixture and milk, alternately, beginning and ending with flour mixture. Blend thoroughly after each addition. Spread batter in prepared pan. Bake at 325° for 90 minutes or until done. Cool 15 minutes before removing from pan.

FROSTING:

4 cups powdered sugar
⅓ cup cocoa
¼ cup margarine, softened

¼ cup evaporated milk
1 teaspoon vanilla
⅛ teaspoon salt

Combine all ingredients till smooth. Frost cool cake.

Lucille Martin, General; Marie Boone, General
(Dogwood Delights)

Black Walnut Coconut Pound Cake

2 cups sugar	½ teaspoon baking powder
1 cup oil	1 cup buttermilk
4 eggs	1 cup chopped black walnuts
3 cups all-purpose flour	1 cup flaked coconut
½ teaspoon salt	2 teaspoons coconut extract
½ teaspoon baking soda	Coconut Syrup

Combine sugar, oil, and eggs; beat till light and frothy. Combine dry ingredients and add to sugar mixture alternately with buttermilk, beating well after each addition. Stir in nuts, coconut, and flavoring. Pour batter into well-greased and floured 10-inch tube pan. Bake at 325° for 1 hour and 5 minutes or till cake tests done. Pour hot Coconut Syrup over hot cake. Allow cake to remain in pan for 4 hours to absorb syrup. Wrap well. Cake will be very moist.

Note: To keep walnuts from sinking, dust them lightly with flour before adding to batter.

COCONUT SYRUP:

1 cup sugar	2 tablespoons butter
½ cup water	1 teaspoon coconut extract

Combine sugar, water, and butter in a saucepan. Bring to a boil for 5 minutes. Remove from heat; stir in flavoring.

Laura Williams, Central (Dogwood Delights II)

Pineapple Pound Cake

½ cup shortening
1 cup butter, softened
2¾ cups sugar
6 eggs
3 cups all-purpose flour

1 teaspoon baking powder
¼ cup milk
1 teaspoon vanilla extract
¾ cup crushed pineapple,
    undrained

Combine shortening, butter, and sugar; cream till light and fluffy. Add eggs, one at a time, beating well after each addition. Combine flour and baking powder; add to creamed mixture alternately with milk and vanilla, beating well after each addition. Stir in crushed pineapple. Pour batter into a well-greased and floured 10-inch tube pan. Place in cold oven; set temperature at 325° and bake 1 hour and 15 minutes. Cool 10–15 minutes in pan. Invert onto serving plate; drizzle Pineapple Glaze over top and sides.

PINEAPPLE GLAZE:

¼ cup butter, melted
1½ cups powdered sugar

1 cup crushed pineapple,
    drained

Combine butter and powdered sugar, mixing until smooth. Blend in pineapple. Drizzle over top and sides of cake.

Millie Banks, W. E.-Region (Dogwood Delights)

Lemon Pound Cake

1 (18¼-ounce) box yellow
   cake mix
1 (3-ounce) box lemon instant
   pudding
1 cup oil

1 cup water
5 eggs
1 cup sugar
1 (6-ounce) can frozen lemon
   concentrate

Combine cake mix and pudding together in large bowl. Blend oil and water into mixture. Add eggs, one at a time, beating well. Pour batter into well-greased tube pan and bake at 350° for 1 hour. Mix sugar and undiluted lemon concentrate; allow to stand at room temperature while cake is baking. Spoon topping over cooled cake.

Pat Lawrence, W. E.-Region (Dogwood Delights)

Blueberry Cake

1 (18¼-ounce) package butter
   cake mix
1 (8-ounce) package cream
   cheese, softened
½ cup sugar
½ cup powdered sugar

1 (9-ounce) carton whipped
   topping
1 teaspoon vanilla
1 (21-ounce) can blueberry pie
   filling

Bake cake according to package directions in 3 layers. Mix cream cheese and sugars; add whipped topping and vanilla. Spread each cake layer with cream cheese mixture, then blueberry pie filling. Ice sides with cream cheese mixture and put blueberries on top only. May substitute any flavor fruit filling.

Ruby Williams, General (Dogwood Delights)

Pineapple Carrot Cake Supreme

CAKE:

2 cups all-purpose flour
2 teaspoons baking powder
1½ teaspoons baking soda
1 teaspoon salt
2 teaspoons cinnamon
1½ cups oil

2 cups sugar
4 eggs
2 cups grated carrots
1 (8-ounce) can crushed
  pineapple, drained
¾ cup chopped pecans

Sift flour, baking powder, baking soda, salt, and cinnamon; set aside. Mix oil, sugar, and eggs; beat well. Add dry ingredients. Slowly blend and mix well. Add carrots, pineapple, and nuts; mix well. Cake batter will be thin. Grease and flour 2 (9-inch) round cake pans. Bake at 325° for about 35 minutes. Test cake with straw or toothpick to be sure center is dry.

ICING:

1 (8-ounce) package cream
  cheese, softened
1 stick margarine, softened
1 (1-pound) box powdered
  sugar, sifted

2 teaspoons vanilla
1 cup chopped pecans
1 cup shredded coconut

Combine cream cheese and margarine in mixing bowl; beat till creamy smooth. Reduce speed of mixer to very low and slowly add sifted sugar until creamy. Blend in vanilla. Add pecans and coconut; mix by hand. Be sure cake has totally cooled before icing.

Elliott H. Gathercoal, General (Dogwood Delights)

Strawberry Cake

1 (18¼-ounce) box white cake
mix
1 (3-ounce) package strawberry
Jell-O

¾ cup oil
4 eggs
1 cup frozen strawberries,
thawed

Mix cake mix, Jell-O, and oil. Add eggs, beating well. Blend in strawberries (use as small amount of liquid in strawberries as possible). Bake in 3 (9-inch) layer pans at 350° for 30–35 minutes.

STRAWBERRY ICING:

1 (1-pound) box powdered
sugar

1 stick margarine, softened
Frozen strawberries

Cream sugar and margarine. Add enough strawberries to reach desired consistency. Spread between layers and ice cake.

Annabelle C. Murden, Decatur, GA (Great Southern Recipes);
Cece Dixon, Austell-Marietta (Dogwood Delights II);
Juanita Hendrix, W.E.-Service/Installations (Dogwood Delights)

The dial telephone was invented by Almon Strowger of St. Louis, Missouri, who patented the automatic telephone exchange in 1891. Mr. Strowger, a mortician, developed the method of direct dialing because he felt exchange operators were diverting his business calls to his competitors. The dial phone was not put into service until 1905 when Dial Switching Equipment was developed. Now, all of this switching equipment has been replaced by computer circuitry.

Apple Cake

1 cup Wesson oil
2 cups sugar
2 eggs
2½ cups all-purpose flour
½ teaspoon salt

1 teaspoon baking soda
2 teaspoons baking powder
1 teaspoon vanilla
1 cup chopped nuts
2 cups diced raw apples

Put oil in bowl; add sugar, eggs, and remaining ingredients except nuts and apples. Stir to mix. Add nuts and apples; mix well. This is a very stiff batter. Bake 1 hour at 325° in greased 8x12-inch pan.

FROSTING:

1 stick butter
½ teaspoon salt

1 cup brown sugar
2 tablespoons evaporated milk

Heat butter in pan. Add remaining ingredients and beat till cool and thick enough to spread. Put on warm cake.

Kitty Stinson, General (Dogwood Delights II)

Orange Slice Cake

1 cup butter, softened
2 cups sugar
4 eggs
½ teaspoon baking soda,
   dissolved in ½ cup
   buttermilk

3½ cups all-purpose flour
1 pound orange slice candies,
   cut in small pieces
1 package dates
2 cups chopped nuts
1 (7-ounce) can flaked coconut

Cream butter and sugar; add eggs one at a time. Add milk mixture and flour; mix well. Roll candy, dates, and nuts in flour. Add with coconut to batter. Grease and flour tube pan, lining only bottom with paper. Cook 2½ hours at 250°.

GLAZE:

1½ cups brown sugar   ½ cup orange juice

Mix well. Pour over hot cake. Leave cake in pan overnight.

Iola Daniel, W. E.-Service/Installation (Dogwood Delights)

Orange Poppy Seed Cake

3 cups unsifted all-purpose
   flour
½ teaspoon salt
1½ teaspoons baking powder
3 eggs
1⅛ cups oil

2¼ cups sugar
1½ cups milk
1½ tablespoons poppy seeds
1½ teaspoons almond flavoring
1½ teaspoons vanilla flavoring
1½ teaspoons butter flavoring

Mix all ingredients with mixer for 2 minutes. Pour into well-greased 10-inch tube pan. Bake at 350° for 1 hour or until done. Top will crack. Let cake cool completely.

FROSTING:

¼ cup orange juice
1 cup powdered sugar
½ teaspoon almond flavoring

½ teaspoon vanilla flavoring
½ teaspoon butter flavoring
1 tablespoon grated orange rind

Mix all ingredients and spread over top. Can be frozen.

Ruth Sutherland, W. E.-Region (Dogwood Delights)

Rave Reviews Coconut Cake

1 (18¼-ounce) box yellow
 cake mix
1 (3-ounce) package vanilla
 instant pudding
1⅓ cups water

4 eggs
¼ cup oil
2 cups flaked coconut
1 cup chopped walnuts or pecans

Blend cake mix, pudding mix, water, eggs, and oil. Beat at medium speed 4 minutes. Stir in coconut and nuts, and pour into 3 greased and floured 9-inch layer pans. Bake at 350° for 35 minutes. Cool and frost.

COCONUT CREAM CHEESE FROSTING:

4 tablespoons margarine,
 divided
2 cups flaked coconut
1 (8-ounce) package cream
 cheese, softened

2 teaspoons milk
3½ cups sifted powdered sugar
½ teaspoon vanilla

Melt 2 tablespoons margarine in skillet; add coconut and stir constantly over low heat till golden brown. Spread coconut on absorbent paper to cool. Cream remaining 2 tablespoons softened margarine with cream cheese; add milk and sugar alternately, beating well. Add vanilla; stir in 1¾ cups coconut. Spread on tops and sides of cake layers. Sprinkle with remaining coconut.

Ruby Williams, General (Dogwood Delights)

Peter Paul Mound Cake

1 (18¼-ounce) box Swiss chocolate cake mix

Bake as directed in 2 pans; cool and split layers.

FILLING:

1 cup sugar
1 cup evaporated milk
1 stick butter

24 large marshmallows
1 (14-ounce) package coconut

Boil hard 2 minutes sugar, milk, and butter together. Remove from heat; add marshmallows and coconut. Spread between layers.

ICING:

1 (1-pound) box powdered
  sugar
½ cup cocoa

¾ cup butter, softened
⅓ cup evaporated milk

Mix ingredients well. Ice top and sides of cake.

Betty Sapp, Chamblee-North Fulton (Dogwood Delights)

Easy Coconut Cake

1 (18¼-ounce) box butter
  cake mix
1½ cups sugar
1 (8-ounce) carton sour cream

1 teaspoon almond flavoring
1 (12-ounce) bag frozen flaked
  coconut, divided
1 (12-ounce) carton Cool Whip

Mix cake and bake in 2 layers according to package directions. When cool, split layers. Mix sugar, sour cream, and flavoring. Add 9 ounces coconut and spread between layers. Mix remaining coconut with Cool Whip. Place on top and sides of cake. Refrigerate. Better if made a day before serving.

Annabelle Murden, Decatur, GA; Kathy Edwards, Chamblee-North Fulton (Great Southern Recipes); Donna Thompson, Athens-Gainesville Council (Lawfully Good Eating) Sara Berry and Rachel Jennings, General (Dogwood Delights)

Italian Cream Cake

1 stick margarine, softened
½ cup shortening
2 cups sugar
5 eggs, separated
2 cups all-purpose flour

1 teaspoon baking soda
1 cup buttermilk
1 teaspoon vanilla
1 (7-ounce) can flaked coconut
1 cup chopped pecans

Cream margarine and shortening; add sugar and beat till smooth. Add egg yolks, one at a time, beating till smooth. Combine flour and baking soda; sift together. Add to creamed mixture alternately with buttermilk. Add vanilla, coconut, and nuts. Fold in stiffly beaten egg whites. Bake in 3 greased 8- or 9-inch pans at 300° for 25 minutes or till done.

FROSTING:

1 (8-ounce) package cream
  cheese, softened
½ stick margarine, softened
1 (1-pound) box powdered
  sugar

1 teaspoon vanilla
Chopped nuts

Beat cream cheese and margarine; add sugar and vanilla. Mix well. Add a little milk, if needed. Spread on cake and sprinkle with nuts.

Bernice D. Heat, Austell-Marietta (Dogwood Delights II); Ruby Williams, General (Dogwood Delights); Maureen Middleton, Athens-Gainesville Council (Lawfully Good Eating)

Hummingbird Cake

3 cups all-purpose flour
2 cups sugar
1 teaspoon salt
1 teaspoon baking soda
1 teaspoon cinnamon
3 eggs, beaten
1½ cups oil

1½ teaspoons vanilla
1 (8-ounce) can crushed
　pineapple, undrained
2 cups chopped pecans or
　walnuts, divided
2 cups chopped bananas

Combine dry ingredients in large bowl; add eggs and oil, stirring until dry ingredients are moistened; do not beat. Stir in vanilla, pineapple, 1 cup chopped nuts, and bananas. Spoon batter into 3 well-greased and floured 9-inch cake pans. Bake at 350° for 25–30 minutes or till cakes are done. Cool in pans 10 minutes. Remove from pans and cool completely. Spread Cream Cheese Frosting between layers and on top and sides; sprinkle with remaining 1 cup chopped nuts.

CREAM CHEESE FROSTING:

1 (8-ounce) package cream
　cheese, softened
½ cup margarine, softened

1 (1-pound) box powdered sugar
1 teaspoon vanilla

Combine all ingredients till smooth.

Mary Smith, Austell-Marietta (Dogwood Delights)

Banana Split Cake

3 sticks margarine, divided
½ pound graham cracker
   crumbs
2 eggs
1 pound powdered sugar
3 large bananas

1 (20-ounce) can crushed
   pineapple, drained
1 (8-ounce) carton whipped
   topping
½ cup sliced cherries
½ cup chopped nuts

Melt 1 stick margarine and stir into cracker crumbs. Press mixture into a 10x14-inch tray or pan. Beat eggs, add remaining softened margarine, then add sugar. Mix several minutes until smooth. Pour over crust. Cover filling with sliced bananas. Then spread on crushed pineapple and whipped topping. Sprinkle with cherries and nuts. Serves 8.

Beckey Gaskamp, Area (Dogwood Delights)

My Mother's Old-Fashioned Jam Cake

½ cup shortening
1¾ cups sugar
3 eggs
2½ cups all-purpose flour
1 cup milk
4 tablespoons cocoa
4 teaspoons baking powder

2 teaspoons cinnamon
1 teaspoon cloves
1 teaspoon nutmeg
1 teaspoon allspice
1–1½ cups blackberry jam or
   jelly
1 cup English walnuts

Cream shortening. Gradually add sugar; cream some more. Add eggs, one at a time, beating after each. Sift all dry ingredients together and add alternately with milk to mixture of shortening, sugar, and eggs. Beat well. Add jam and nuts, stir in well. Bake in a lightly greased tube or Bundt pan at 325° for 1 hour. Test with straw in middle to be sure it is done.

Margie Linnartz, Brookwood-Downtown (Dogwood Delights)

St. Patrick's Green or Red Velvet Cake

CAKE:

2 eggs
1½ cups sugar
1¼ cups oil
1 teaspoon vinegar
2½ cups self-rising flour

1 teaspoon baking soda
1 cup buttermilk
1 teaspoon vanilla
1 (1-ounce) bottle green or red
  food coloring

Beat eggs in mixer; add sugar, oil, and vinegar, then blend well. Sift flour and baking soda together and add to egg mixture alternately with buttermilk. Blend ingredients well, then add vanilla and food coloring. Pour batter into 3 (8-inch) cake pans which have been greased and floured. Bake at 350° for 25 minutes. Cool before frosting.

FROSTING:

1 (8-ounce) package cream
  cheese
1 stick margarine

1 (1-pound) box powdered sugar
1 teaspoon vanilla
Chopped pecans

Place cream cheese and butter in top of double boiler. Melt over low heat. Add powdered sugar and blend well. Add flavoring and pecans as desired. Frost cake when cool. Use bright red for Christmas or green for St. Patrick's Day.

Marvella Garriss, Chamblee-North Fulton (Dogwood Delights);
Cindy Channell, Chamblee-North Fulton (Dogwood Delights II)

Pumpkin Cake Roll

3 eggs
1 cup sugar
⅔ cup cooked pumpkin
1 teaspoon lemon juice
¾ cup all-purpose flour
1 teaspoon baking powder

2 teaspoons cinnamon
1 teaspoon ginger
½ teaspoon nutmeg
½ teaspoon salt
1 cup finely chopped nuts

Beat eggs on high speed 5 minutes. Gradually add sugar and beat until smooth. Stir in pumpkin and lemon juice. Fold flour, baking powder, spices, and salt into mixture. Spread in a greased and floured 10x15-inch pan. Top with chopped nuts. Bake at 375° for 15 minutes.

Turn out on a towel sprinkled with powdered sugar. Starting at the narrow end, roll towel and cake together. Cool an hour or so. Unroll and spread Filling on cake. Roll up again with out towel. Chill before serving. Freezes well.

FILLING:

1 (8-ounce) package cream
  cheese, softened
4 tablespoons butter, softened

1 cup powdered sugar
1 teaspoon vanilla

Combine cream cheese and butter; add sugar and vanilla. Spread on cake.

Gerene Leffingwell, Brookwood-Downtown (Dogwood Delights)

Peanut Butter Cake

1 (18¼-ounce) box yellow
   cake mix
1½ cups sugar
¼ stick butter, softened

2 heaping tablespoons peanut
   butter
½ cup milk
1 teaspoon vanilla

Make cake in 3 layers according to package directions. Mix sugar, butter, peanut butter, and milk in saucepan; cook approximately 6 minutes after mixture starts to boil. Let cool, then add vanilla and spread on cake layers.

Mike Hicks, Marietta, GA (Great Southern Recipes)

Coca-Cola Cake

2 cups unsifted all-purpose
   flour
2 cups sugar
2 tablespoons cocoa
1 teaspoon salt
1 teaspoon baking soda

2 sticks margarine
1 cup Coca-Cola
½ cup buttermilk
2 eggs
1½ cups miniature
   marshmallows

Combine flour, sugar, cocoa, salt, and baking soda. Bring butter and Coke to a boil. Add to dry ingredients. Add buttermilk, eggs, and marshmallows. Mix well. Bake in greased 9x13-inch pan at 350° for 45 minutes.

ICING:

½ cup margarine, melted
2 tablespoons cocoa
6 tablespoons Coca-Cola

1 (1-pound) box powdered
   sugar
1 teaspoon vanilla

Mix all ingredients together. Pour over hot cake.

Barbara Elliott, W. E.-Service/Installation (Dogwood Delights)

Cherry-Chocolate Cake

1 ounce unsweetened chocolate
2 cups all-purpose flour
1 cup sugar
1 teaspoon baking soda
¼ teaspoon salt
½ cup shortening
¾ cup milk

¼ cup maraschino cherry juice
  (reserve remainder)
2 eggs
½ cup chopped maraschino
  cherries
Several drops red food coloring

Grease and flour 2 (9-inch) cake pans; set aside. Preheat oven to 350°. Melt chocolate; set aside. In large mixer bowl, combine flour, sugar, baking soda, and salt. Make a well in center of flour mixture. Drop in shortening, milk, cherry juice, and eggs. Blend with electric mixer on low speed, then beat on medium speed 2 minutes. Add melted chocolate, cherries, and food coloring. Beat another minute. Pour into prepared pans. Bake 25–30 minutes or till done. Cool in pans 10 minutes. Turn out on wire racks. Cool completely. Spread Cherry-Chocolate Frosting on cake. Makes 1 (2-layer, 9-inch) cake.

CHERRY-CHOCOLATE FROSTING:
1 ounce unsweetened chocolate
½ cup butter or margarine,
  softened
3 cups sifted powdered sugar

¼ cup maraschino cherry juice
½ cup chopped maraschino
  cherries

Melt chocolate; set aside. In small mixer bowl, cream butter or margarine. Add powdered sugar and cherry juice. Beat till smooth. Stir in melted chocolate and cherries. Frost cake.

Lorine Harris, General (Dogwood Delights)

Deep Dark Chocolate Cake

1¾ cups unsifted all-purpose
   flour
¾ cup cocoa
2 cups sugar
1½ teaspoons baking soda
1½ teaspoons baking powder

1 teaspoon salt
1 cup milk
2 eggs
½ cup oil
2 teaspoons vanilla
1 cup boiling water

Combine dry ingredients in large mixing bowl. Add remaining ingredients except boiling water; beat at medium speed 2 minutes. Remove from mixer; stir in boiling water; batter will be thin. Pour into 2 greased and floured (9-inch) or 3 (8-inch) layer pans or 1 (9x13-inch) pan. Bake at 350° for 30–35 minutes for layers, 35–40 minutes for 9x13, or till cake tester comes out clean. Cool 10 minutes on rack. Remove from pans; cool completely. Top with Chocolate Frosting.

CHOCOLATE FROSTING:

¾ cup cocoa
4 cups powdered sugar
½ cup butter, softened

½ cup evaporated milk
1 teaspoon vanilla

Mix cocoa and sugar; cream with butter. Blend in milk and vanilla. Beat till smooth and creamy.

Joan Moore, General (Dogwood Delights)

German Chocolate Upside-Down Cake

In spite of the name, this cake cannot be inverted onto a platter because the gooey bottom that makes it so delicious also makes it stick to the pan. However, individual slices can be served upside down.

1 cup shredded coconut
1 cup chopped pecans
1 (18¼-ounce) box German
  chocolate cake mix
1 stick margarine, softened

1 (8-ounce) package cream
  cheese, softened
1 (1-pound) package powdered
  sugar

Mix together coconut and nuts; put into bottom of greased 9x13-inch pan. Prepare cake mix according to directions on box and pour over coconut-pecan mixture.

Place margarine and cream cheese in a saucepan; heat till mixture is warm; stir in powdered sugar. Spoon over top of cake mix. Bake 35–40 minutes at 350°. Do not cut till cool. Makes 1 sheet cake.

Pam Mennella, General (Dogwood Delights II)

Mississippi Mud Cake

2 sticks butter
½ cup cocoa
4 eggs, well beaten
1½ cups all-purpose flour

2 cups sugar
Dash of salt
1½ cups chopped pecans
1 small package marshmallows

Melt butter; add cocoa, eggs, flour, sugar, and salt; mix well. Pour into greased and floured oblong cake pan. Bake at 350° for 35 minutes or till sides turn loose from pan. Sprinkle marshmallows over hot cake.

ICING:
1 (1-pound) box powdered
   sugar
⅓ cup cocoa

½ stick butter, softened
½ cup milk
½ teaspoon vanilla

Combine all ingredients; beat well. Pour over hot cake.

Sandy Saxton, General; Betty Long, Brookwood-Downtown
(Dogwood Delights); Mary Mims, Columbus Life Member Club
(Lawfully Good Eating) (Dogwood Delights II)

Butterscotch Cake

2 eggs
1 can butterscotch pudding
1 (18¼-ounce) box yellow cake
   mix

1 (12-ounce) package butterscotch bits
1 cup chopped pecans

Beat eggs lightly. Add pudding and cake mix. Blend till smooth. Pour mixture into lightly greased and floured 9x13-inch pan. Sprinkle bits and nuts on top. Press into batter lightly. Bake at 350° for 35–40 minutes. Test for doneness.

Violetta Hyland, Jonesboro-South Fulton (Dogwood Delights II)

Éclair Cake

2 (3-ounce) packages French
   vanilla instant pudding mix
3 cups cold milk

1 (8-ounce) carton Cool Whip
1 box graham crackers

Mix pudding with milk; let set 15 minutes. Then mix with Cool Whip. Put one layer of graham crackers in a greased 9x12-inch pan. Top with ½ of pudding mixture and another layer of graham crackers, the rest of the pudding mixture and another layer of graham crackers.

FROSTING:

1½ cups powdered sugar
3 tablespoons margarine,
   softened
3 tablespoons milk

2 ounces unsweetened chocolate,
   melted
2 tablespoons white Karo syrup
1 tablespoon vanilla

Mix thoroughly, spread over cake, and refrigerate overnight.

Joanne Ross, General (Dogwood Delights)

The mobile telephone was invented by Bell Telephone Company and introduced into New York City police cars in 1924. Although the first commercial mobile telephone service became available in St. Louis, Missouri, in 1946, the mobile telephone would not become common for another four decades.

Punch Bowl Cake

1 (18¼-ounce) box white or
  yellow cake mix
1 (6-ounce) package vanilla
  instant pudding
1 (12-ounce) carton Cool Whip

1 (20-ounce) can crushed
  pineapple, drained
1 (21-ounce) can cherry pie
  filling
Chopped nuts

Bake cake according to package directions. Crumble one layer in punch bowl. Mix pudding with ½ cup more milk than called for on package. Pour half over cake. Spread with half the pineapple. Spread with half the cherry pie filling. Spread with half the Cool Whip. Spread with finely chopped nuts. Repeat layers. Refrigerate overnight.

Note: When making first layer, use a little less than half, because you will need more as the bowl gets larger at the top.

Ellen Manley, General (Dogwood Delights II); Pearlean Sheffield,
Austell-Marietta (Dogwood Delights)

Chocoholics'
Chocolate Cheesecake

CRUMB CRUST:

1 (8½-ounce) package
   chocolate wafers
⅓ cup butter, melted

2 tablespoons sugar
¼ teaspoon nutmeg

Preheat oven to 350°. Crush chocolate wafers in blender or with rolling pin till fine crumbs. Combine crumbs, melted butter, sugar, and nutmeg. Press into springform pan on bottom and sides to ½ inch from top. Refrigerate.

CHEESE FILLING:

3 eggs
1 cup sugar
3 (8-ounce) packages cream
   cheese, softened
1 (12-ounce) package semisweet
   chocolate chips, melted

1 teaspoon vanilla
⅛ teaspoon salt
1 cup sour cream

Beat eggs with sugar on high speed till light; beat in cream cheese till smooth. Add melted chocolate, vanilla, salt, and sour cream. Beat till smooth. Pour mixture into Crumb Crust.

Bake 1 hour or until cheesecake is just firm when pan is shaken. Do not overbake. Cool on wire rack, then refrigerate, covered, overnight. Serve with whipped cream decorations, if desired. Serves 16.

Marilyn Jeffries, General (Dogwood Delights)

Cherry Cheese Cake

½ (8-ounce) package cream
  cheese, softened
1 cup powdered sugar
Dash of salt (optional)
½ teaspoon vanilla

1 cup whipping cream
1 (9-inch) pie shell, baked
1 (21-ounce) can cherry pie
  filling

Cream cheese; add powdered sugar, salt, and vanilla; mix well.
Beat whipping cream till quite stiff. Fold into cream cheese. Pour
into baked pie shell. Cover with cherry pie filling. Chill and serve.

Denni Coker, General (Dogwood Delights)

Lisa's Mini Cheese Cakes

2 (8-ounce) packages cream
  cheese, softened
½ cup sugar

1 teaspoon vanilla
2 eggs
12 vanilla wafers

Mix cream cheese, sugar, and vanilla till well blended, then add
eggs and mix well. Put vanilla wafers in foil liners in muffin pan.
Fill each cup ¾ cup full and bake in 325° oven 25 minutes.

Lisa Neville, Decatur-Tucker (Dogwood Delights II)

New York Style Cheesecake

CRUST:

1½ cups graham cracker
  crumbs

¼ cup sugar

6 tablespoons butter, melted

Combine crumbs and sugar; add melted butter and mix to moisten. Press mixture on bottom and part way up sides of a 10-inch springform pan. Place in refrigerator to chill while making Filling.

FILLING:

5 (8-ounce) packages cream
  cheese, softened

3 tablespoons all-purpose flour

1¾ cups sugar

3 tablespoons vanilla

3 tablespoons fresh lemon juice

5 whole eggs plus 2 egg yolks

¼ cup whipping cream

Preheat oven to 500°. Cream cheese with mixer till soft and fluffy. Beat in flour; beat in sugar a little at a time. Beat in vanilla, lemon juice, eggs and egg yolks one at a time, beating very well between additions. Pour cheese mixture into prepared springform pan. Bake at 500° for 12 minutes. Turn oven down to 200° and bake 45 minutes, depending on oven; be sure center is firm, not mushy, before proceeding to next step.

Turn oven off and leave cake in oven 15 minutes. Remove pan from oven and cool on rack 1 hour. Refrigerate cake in pan 5 hours before removing side of pan. This is very important; the cake may collapse if the 5-hour period is cut short. Serves 20.

Ed Bingham, W. E.-Service/Installation (Dogwood Delights)

Fudgy Chocolate Frosting

½ cup cocoa
2 cups sugar
1 stick margarine, softened

½ cup milk
½ teaspoon vanilla

Place all ingredients in large iron skillet; bring to a boil, stirring constantly. Cook for 2–3 minutes.

Helen Dover, W. E.-Region (Dogwood Delights); Lagita Kirk,
Austell-Marietta (Dogwood Delights II)

Tasty Icing

½ cup shortening
1 (1-pound) box powdered
   sugar, sifted

Dash of salt
¼ cup water
Flavoring (optional)

Place shortening into large mixing bowl and blend briefly. Sift in the sugar and salt; begin mixing and add water gradually as the frosting blends. Add flavoring, if desired.

Kittie Mae Russell, Brookwood-Downtown (Dogwood Delights)

Cream Cheese Icing

1 stick butter, softened
1 (8-ounce) package cream
   cheese, softened
1 teaspoon vanilla

1 (1-pound) box powdered
   sugar
1 egg yolk

Beat butter and cream cheese with mixer till fluffy, 3–5 minutes. Add vanilla and powdered sugar. Add egg yolk, beat till fluffy.

Peytie Halligan, Chamblee-North Fulton (Dogwood Delights II)

Cookies and Candies

1968
Trimline

The twelve-button Touch-Tone Trimline was dramatically different from any other phone at the time. With the first ever dial-in-handset, it allowed people to dial a new call without returning to the base of the phone. The design of the phone later paved the way for today's cordless and cellular phones. Although only ten buttons were needed for ordinary dialing, the two "extra" buttons (the * and # keys) were added for advanced services and for dialing international phone calls. The first Touch-Tone Trimline phone had round buttons instead of square. The convenience of having the dial in the handset was especially handy in the wall-mount model. The Trimline model also introduced the concept of modular plugs. Also in 1968, 911 was introduced as a nationwide emergency number.

Butter Cookies

2 eggs
1¼ cup powdered sugar
3 stick butter, softened

4 cups all-purpose flour
1 teaspoon vanilla
Sprinkles

Beat eggs and sugar till fluffy. Add butter, flour, and vanilla. Put dough through a cookie press onto wax paper. Scatter sprinkles over dough generously. Cut strips into individual cookies. Bake at 350° on greased cookie sheet till golden brown, 5–8 minutes.

Mickey Fennelly, W. E.-Service/Installation (Dogwood Delights)

Grandma Ruth's Oatmeal Cookies

1 cup butter, softened
1 cup sugar
1 cup brown sugar
2 eggs
1 teaspoon vanilla
2½ cups all-purpose flour

1 teaspoon baking soda
¾ teaspoon salt
2 cups quick-cooking oats
Raisins or nuts to taste
    (optional)

Cream butter, sugar, and brown sugar; add eggs, and mix well. Add vanilla, and mix well. Add flour, baking soda, and salt. Mix well. Add oats and raisins or nuts, if desired. Form balls and place on greased cookie sheet. Bake at 375° for 10–12 minutes. Makes 4 dozen.

Carrie M. Lampkin, Conyers, GA (Great Southern Recipes)

Oatmeal Cookies

1 cup shortening
¾ cup brown sugar
¾ cup white sugar
1 or 2 eggs (depending on size)
1 teaspoon cinnamon
1 teaspoon vanilla
¼ teaspoon salt
½ teaspoon baking soda
¼ cup water (less if 2 eggs are used)
1 cup all-purpose flour
3½ cups oatmeal

Cream shortening, sugars, and eggs. Add spices; mix. Add salt, baking soda, water, and flour; mix. Stir in oatmeal a little at a time till all blended. Drop by teaspoon onto cookie sheet. Bake at 400° for 8–10 minutes (8 for chewy; 10 for crunchy).

Marsha Sahlman, General (Dogwood Delights)

Scotcheroos

1 cup peanut butter
1 cup light corn syrup
1 cup sugar
2 cups butterscotch chips, divided
6 cups crisp rice cereal
2 cups semisweet chocolate chips

Combine peanut butter, corn syrup, sugar, and ¼ cup butterscotch chips in saucepan. Cook over medium-high heat till peanut butter is softened. Pour over cereal in bowl; mix well. Pat into 9x13-inch dish. Melt chocolate chips and remaining 1¾ cups butterscotch chips in bowl in microwave. Pour over cereal mixture. Chill till firm. Cut into squares. Yields 15 servings.

Myra Poole, Gainesville Life Member Club
(Lawfully Good Eating)

Pecan Surprise Bars

1 (18¼-ounce) package yellow
   cake mix
½ cup butter, melted
4 eggs, divided

1½ cups dark corn syrup
1 teaspoon vanilla extract
½ cup packed brown sugar
1 cup chopped pecans

Reserve ⅔ cup cake mix. Combine remaining cake mix, melted butter, and 1 egg in bowl; mix well with fork. Spread in greased baking pan. Bake at 350° for 15 minutes, or till golden brown. Combine reserved cake mix, corn syrup, remaining 3 eggs, vanilla, and brown sugar in bowl; mix well. Stir in pecans. Pour over crust. Bake at 350° for 30–35 minutes, or till brown. Cool in pan. Cut into bars. Yields 15 servings.

Anita Smith, Athens-Gainesville Council (Lawfully Good Eating)

Lester Williams' Christmas Cookies

1 cup butter, softened
3 eggs, well beaten
1–2 teaspoons cinnamon
½ cup sherry or milk
1 cup packed brown sugar
½ teaspoon baking soda

3 cups all-purpose flour
7 cups chopped pecans
1 pound each: dates, candied
   cherries, and candied
   pineapple, chopped
½ pound raisins

Mix first 7 ingredients in bowl. Stir in pecans, dates, cherries, pineapple, and raisins. Drop by spoonfuls onto greased cookie sheet. Bake at 300° for 20 minutes, or till brown. Cool on cookie sheet several minutes. Remove to wire rack to cool. Yields 100 cookies.

Faye Richey, Augusta Council (Lawfully Good Eating)

Nut Crescents

5 cups cake flour, sifted	4½ cups chopped pecans
2 cups butter, softened	1 cup powdered sugar
¼ cup vanilla extract	

Combine flour and butter in bowl; mix well. Stir in vanilla and pecans. Shape into small crescents. Place on nonstick baking sheet. Bake at 350° for 12–15 minutes, or till brown. Roll warm cookies 4 times in powdered sugar. Store in refrigerator. Yields 120 cookies.

Sheila Burkes, Columbus Council (Lawfully Good Eating)

Savannah Sand Bars

1 stick butter, softened	½ cup chopped nuts
¼ cup sugar	1 teaspoon vanilla
1 cup all-purpose flour	

Cream butter; add sugar, stir. Add flour. (This process may be done in food processor.) Add nuts and vanilla. Drop on ungreased cookie sheet by ½ teaspoon. Bake at 300° about 30 minutes. When cookies cool, sprinkle with powdered sugar.

Brenda Plunkett, General (Dogwood Delights II)

Pecan Tassies

CHEESE PASTRY:

1 (3-ounce) package cream
  cheese, softened

½ cup butter, softened
1 cup sifted all-purpose flour

Combine cream cheese and butter; stir in flour and chill 1 hour. Shape into 2 dozen 1-inch balls. Press dough against bottoms and sides of small muffin pans, making shell.

PECAN FILLING:

1 egg
¾ cup brown sugar
1 tablespoon butter

1 teaspoon vanilla
Dash of salt
⅔ cup chopped pecans, divided

Beat together egg, sugar, butter, vanilla, and salt. Divide ½ nuts among shells. Add egg-brown sugar mixture and top with remaining pecans. Bake in slow 325° oven 25 minutes, or till mixture is set. Cool and remove from pans.

Sandra Garrett, Austell-Marietta (Dogwood Delights II)

Tea Cakes

1½ cups sugar
½ cup butter, softened
½ cup shortening

1 teaspoon vanilla
2 eggs
3 cups self-rising flour

Mix everything, adding flour 1 cup at a time. Drop onto cookie sheet. Bake at 350° till brown.

Janet Miles, Austell-Marietta (Dogwood Delights II)

Diabetic Cookies

1 square unsweetened chocolate
¼ cup milk
1 stick margarine
1 box chopped raisins
1 box ground dates

1 cup chopped nuts
½ cup peanut butter
1 teaspoon liquid sweetener
3 cups quick oatmeal
1 teaspoon vanilla

Cook chocolate, milk, and margarine for 1 minute. Stir while cooking. Add remaining ingredients and mix with hands. Roll into walnut-size balls. Do not bake. Can be frozen. Makes 40 cookies.

Eunice Thompson, Perimeter (Dogwood Delights II)

Peanut Blossoms

1 cup sugar
1 cup brown sugar
1 cup butter, softened
1 cup peanut butter
2 eggs
¼ cup milk

2 teaspoons vanilla
3½ cups all-purpose flour
2 teaspoons baking soda
1 teaspoon salt
2 (10-ounce) packages chocolate
    kisses, peeled

Cream sugars, butter, and peanut butter. Beat in eggs, milk, and vanilla. Sift together dry ingredients and stir into egg mixture. Shape into 1-inch balls and roll in additional sugar. Place on ungreased cookie sheet. Bake at 375° for 10–12 minutes. Remove from oven and immediately press a chocolate kiss in center of each cookie. Let cool.

Carol Bass, Area (Dogwood Delights II)

The Ultimate Chocolate Chip Cookie

¾ cup butter-flavored Crisco
1¼ cups firmly packed brown sugar
2 tablespoons milk
1 tablespoon vanilla
1 egg

1¾ cups all-purpose flour
1 teaspoon salt
¾ teaspoon baking soda
1 cup semisweet chocolate chips or chunks
1 cup pecan pieces

Heat oven to 375°. Cream Crisco, brown sugar, milk, and vanilla in large bowl. Blend till creamy. Beat in egg. Combine flour, salt, and baking soda; add to creamed mixture gradually. Stir in chocolate chips and nuts. Drop by rounded tablespoons 3 inches apart on ungreased baking sheet. Bake at 375° for 8–10 minutes for chewy cookies and 11–13 minutes for crispy cookies. Cool on baking sheet 2 minutes. Remove and cool on cooling rack.

Pat Gulley, Decatur-Tucker (Dogwood Delights II)

The first Picturephone test system, built in 1956, was crude—it transmitted an image only once every two seconds. By 1964 a complete experimental system, the "Mod 1," had been developed, but failed miserably. It wasn't until decades later, with improvements in speed, resolution, miniaturization, and the incorporation of Picturephone into another piece of desktop equipment, the computer, that the promise of a personal video communication system was realized.

Santa's Surprise

2 sticks butter, softened	3½ cups all-purpose flour
1 cup creamy peanut butter	1 teaspoon baking soda
1 cup light brown sugar	½ teaspoon salt
2 eggs	1 large bag miniature Snickers
1 teaspoon vanilla	1 bag Dove milk chocolate candy

Combine first 3 ingredients, using mixer, till light and fluffy. Slowly add eggs and vanilla till thoroughly combined. Mix in flour, baking soda, and salt. Cover and chill dough 2 or 3 hours.

Preheat oven to 350°. Unwrap Snickers as needed. Remove dough from refrigerator. Take one tablespoon cookie dough and wrap around a Snickers. Form into a ball. Place on greased cookie sheet and bake 10–12 minutes. Let cookies cool on baking rack. Melt Dove chocolate (does not take a whole bag) and drizzle over cookies. Makes 3–4 dozen cookies.

Brenda Harris, Loganville, GA (Great Southern Recipes)

Crunchy Peanut Butter Drops

1 cup light corn syrup	2 cups peanut butter
1 cup sugar	4 cups cornflakes

In large saucepan over medium heat, cook and stir corn syrup and sugar 7–8 minutes, or till sugar is dissolved (do not boil). Remove from heat; add peanut butter; mix well. Fold in cornflakes.

Drop by rounded tablespoonfuls onto wax paper coated with nonstick cooking spray. Let sit 1½–2 hours, or till set. Store in wax paper-lined airtight container. Yields 3½ dozen.

Gail S. Kirkpatrick, Conyers, GA (Great Southern Recipes)

Peanut Butter Cookies

½ cup margarine, softened
½ teaspoon vanilla
½ cup peanut butter
½ cup brown sugar, firmly
  packed

½ cup sugar
1 egg
½ cup sifted all-purpose flour
1 teaspoon baking soda
½ teaspoon salt

Cream margarine, vanilla, and peanut butter till well blended. Add sugars; cream thoroughly. Add egg and beat well. Sift together flour, baking soda, and salt. Add to sugar mixture and blend well. Roll into small balls ½ inch in diameter. Place on cookie sheet 2 inches apart. Press with fork. Bake at 375° for 10–12 minutes or till lightly browned.

Cecile Cram, Chamblee-North Fulton (Dogwood Delights)

Ginger Snaps

2¼ cups all-purpose flour
¾ cup oil
¼ cup molasses
¼ cup maple syrup
2 teaspoons baking soda
1 teaspoon ground ginger

½ teaspoon ground cinnamon
½ teaspoon ground cardamom
¼ teaspoon salt
1 egg
½ cup sugar

Combine all ingredients in large bowl. Beat till well blended, occasionally scraping bowl. Place 2 tablespoons sugar on wax paper. Shape dough into balls and roll in sugar to coat evenly. Place balls 3 inches apart on ungreased cookie sheet. Bake at 350° for 15 minutes.

Cynthia Milford, General (Dogwood Delights)

Mother's Fruitcake Cookies

1 cup butter, softened
1 cup brown sugar
3 eggs, well beaten
3 cups all-purpose flour
1 teaspoon baking soda
1 teaspoon cinnamon
½ cup milk
2 cups candied fruitcake mix

1 cup candied cherries, cut in
   small pieces
1 box (about 2 cups) chopped
   dates
¾ box raisins
4 cups chopped pecans
1 teaspoon vanilla

Cream butter and sugar; add eggs. Mix dry ingredients in separate bowl. Add alternately with milk to creamed mixture. Add fruit and nuts, one ingredient at a time, stirring after each addition. Add vanilla; stir. Drop onto cookie sheet that has been sprayed with Pam. Bake 20–30 minutes at 300°.

Note: Makes between 6 and 8 dozen, depending on size of cookie. These can be stored at room temperature in air tight container and will keep for weeks.

Susan Sloan, Fayetteville, GA (Great Southern Recipes)

Chess Bars

1 (18¼-ounce) package yellow
   cake mix
1 cup chopped pecans
4 eggs, divided
1 stick butter, softened

1 (8-ounce) package cream
   cheese, softened
1 (1-pound) box powdered
   sugar
¼ teaspoon salt

Combine cake mix, nuts, 1 egg, and butter in a 9x13-inch pan. Mix with hands and press down in pan. Combine cream cheese, remaining 3 eggs, sugar, and salt. Mix with mixer till smooth and creamy. Pour over cake mixture. Bake 35–50 minutes at 350°. Cool completely before cutting.

Pat Gulley, Decatur-Tucker (Dogwood Delights II)

Lemon-Cheese Squares

3 eggs, divided
½ cup butter
1 cup chopped pecans
1 (18¼-ounce) package
pudding-recipe lemon cake
mix

1 (1-pound) package powdered
sugar
1 (8-ounce) package cream
cheese, softened

Cut 1 egg, butter, and pecans into cake mix in bowl. Spread on large baking sheet. Combine powdered sugar, remaining 2 eggs, and cream cheese; mix well. Spoon over pecan mixture. Bake at 325° for 30–35 minutes, or till light brown. Yields 15 servings.

Lucy Parmer, Columbus Council (Lawfully Good Eating)

Lemon Slices

2 cups all-purpose flour
1 cup butter, melted

½ cup powdered sugar

Combine ingredients and cream together. Pat into a 9x13-inch pan sprayed with Pam. Bake 20–25 minutes at 350°.

4 eggs
2 cups sugar
¼ cup bottled lemon juice

4 tablespoons all-purpose flour
¼ teaspoon salt
Powdered sugar

Combine all ingredients except powdered sugar. Pour over baked crust. Bake again at 350° for 25 minutes. While still warm, sprinkle with powdered sugar. When completely cool, slice and serve.

Barbara Paris, Austell-Mairetta (Dogwood Delights II)

Chocolate Caramel Brownies

1 bag caramel candies
⅔ cup evaporated milk,
  divided
1 (18¼-ounce) box German
  chocolate cake mix

¾ cup margarine, melted
½ teaspoon vanilla
1 (12-ounce) bag chocolate chips
1 cup chopped pecans
Pecan halves (optional)

Mix caramels and ⅓ cup evaporated milk in small saucepan and cook till caramels have melted. Mix cake mix, remaining ⅓ cup milk, margarine, and vanilla together.

Grease and flour a 9x13-inch cake pan, and place ½ of cake mixture in pan. Bake at 350° for 6 minutes, then pour chocolate chips, melted caramel mix, and chopped nuts over top. Put rest of cake mixture on top and bake 25 minutes at 350°. Put pecan halves on top, if desired.

Jerry Farkas, Marietta, GA (Great Southern Recipes)

Chocolate Covered
Peanut Butter Balls

2 sticks butter, softened
1 (1-pound) box powdered sugar
  plus 1 cup
¾ cup crunchy peanut butter

1 (6-ounce) package chocolate
  morsels
½ bar paraffin

Cream butter, sugar, and peanut butter. Roll into balls. Melt chocolate morsels and paraffin in double boiler. Insert toothpick into ball and dip in chocolate. Place on wax paper to dry.

Pat Gulley, Decatur-Tucker (Dogwood Delights II)

Georgia Nuggets

3 cups light brown sugar
1 cup cream
½ teaspoon vanilla

1 tablespoon butter
2 cups chopped pecans

Stir sugar and cream together in saucepan till sugar is dissolved. Bring to boiling point and cook to 232° or till candy forms soft ball when tried in water. Remove from heat. When cool, add vanilla, butter, and nuts. Beat till creamy. Drop on wax paper.

Polly Templeton, Area (Dogwood Delights II)

French Meringue Kisses

2 egg whites
⅛ teaspoon salt
⅛ teaspoon cream of tartar

½ cup sugar
½ teaspoon vanilla
½ cup mini chocolate chips

Beat egg whites, salt, and cream of tartar till egg whites are stiff, but not dry. Beat in sugar, a little at a time. Fold in vanilla and chips.

Drop by teaspoonfuls on ungreased parchment paper. Bake at 275° for 40–60 minutes. Makes about 2 dozen kisses. They will keep for a long time in tightly covered can.

Phyllis Yancey, Decatur, GA (Great Southern Recipes)

Coconut Orange Balls

1½ cups powdered sugar
⅓ cup orange juice
  concentrate

¼ cup butter, softened
8 ounces vanilla wafers, crushed
⅔ cup shredded coconut

Cream sugar, orange juice concentrate, and butter. Mix in vanilla wafers. Shape into balls and roll in coconut. Makes 3½ dozen.

Pat Gulley, Decatur Tucker (Dogwood Delights II)

Pecan Balls

1 cup butter, softened
4 tablespoons sugar
2 teaspoons vanilla

2 cups all-purpose flour
2 cups chopped pecans
Powdered sugar

Cream butter and sugar; add vanilla, flour, and nuts. Roll into small balls. Bake 20 minutes at 300°. Roll balls in powdered sugar immediately after taking them out of oven.

Mrs. Joseph (Mickey) M. Fennelly, W. E.-Service/Installation
(Dogwood Delights)

Turtles

78 caramel candies
2 tablespoons margarine
2 tablespoons evaporated milk
2 cups pecan halves

2 (12-ounce) packages milk
 chocolate chips
¼ block paraffin

Heat first 3 ingredients in top of double boiler until smooth (or 5 minutes in microwave). Stir in pecans. Drop by spoonful on buttered cookie sheets. Refrigerate till cool.

Melt chocolate chips and paraffin in top of double boiler. Dip caramels into chocolate mixture. Keep chocolate mixture warm while dipping.

Betty Wright, Jonesboro-South Fulton (Dogwood Delights)

New Orleans Pralines

3 cups sugar, divided
1 cup light cream
¼ teaspoon salt

2 tablespoons butter
2 teaspoons vanilla
2 cups pecan halves

Combine 2 cups sugar, light cream, salt, and butter in large, heavy saucepan over low heat, stirring often. In a small, heavy saucepan, melt remaining 1 cup sugar over low heat. Pour melted sugar into hot sugar-cream mixture very slowly, stirring constantly. Cook until candy thermometer registers 235° or soft-ball stage. Remove from heat and stir in vanilla and nuts. Beat or stir until mixture begins to thicken. Drop rounded teaspoons onto foil or wax paper; cool.

Joyce Teasley, General (Dogwood Delights)

Butterfingers

Peanut butter
2 cups sugar
1 cup light corn syrup

½ cup water
Chocolate chips
Paraffin

Spread peanut butter in bottom of cast-iron skillet. Set aside. Combine sugar, corn syrup, and water in saucepan. Cook over high heat to 290° on candy thermometer, soft-crack stage. Pour over peanut butter; mix well. Spread on lightly buttered baking sheet. Melt chocolate chips with paraffin in double boiler. Pour over candy. Let stand till cool. Cut into bite-size pieces. Yields 16 servings.

Maureen Middleton, Athens-Gainesville Council
(Lawfully Good Eating)

Martha Washington Candy

½ cup margarine, softened
1 (14-ounce) can condensed
    milk
4 cups chopped pecans
1 (3-ounce) can flaked coconut

2 (1-pound) packages
    powdered sugar
2 cups chocolate chips
¾ square paraffin

Combine margarine, condensed milk, pecans, coconut, and powdered sugar in large bowl; mix well. Drop by teaspoonfuls onto wax paper. Melt chocolate and paraffin in top of double boiler over hot water; mix well. Dip candy into chocolate. Let stand till set. Store in refrigerator. Yields 50 servings.

Mary Culpepper, Columbus Council (Lawfully Good Eating)

Taffy

1 bottle dark corn syrup
2 cups sugar

½ cup margarine
1 cup flaked coconut or nuts

Combine corn syrup, sugar, and margarine in deep saucepan. Bring to a boil over high heat to 250°–268° on candy thermometer, hard-ball stage. Remove from heat. Stir in coconut or nuts. Pour into buttered dish. Let stand till cool. Break into pieces. Yields 18 servings.

Stella Malloy, Athens-Gainesville Council
(Lawfully Good Eating)

Bulldog Brittle

8 whole graham crackers
1 cup chopped pecans
½ cup margarine

½ cup butter
½ cup sugar

Break graham crackers into fourths. Place in foil-lined 10x15-inch baking pan, leaving space between crackers. Sprinkle pecans over top. Melt margarine and butter in top of double boiler. Add sugar. Bring to a boil, stirring constantly. Boil 2 minutes exactly. Pour over graham crackers and pecans. Bake at 350° for 10–12 minutes. Let stand till cool. Break into pieces. Yields 32 servings.

Billy Oglesby, Oconee Council (Lawfully Good Eating)

Peanut Brittle Candy

2 cups sugar
1 cup white Karo
½ cup water
3 cups raw peanuts

2 teaspoons baking soda
2 tablespoons butter
1 teaspoon vanilla
1 teaspoon salt

Boil sugar, Karo, and water till mixture reaches 235° on candy thermometer. Add peanuts; boil to 290°. Remove from heat. Add baking soda, butter, vanilla, and salt. Stir well. Pour onto buttered pan and cool. Bread into pieces and store in airtight containers.

Randy Pearson, General (Dogwood Delights II)

Brazil Nut Fudge

2 cups sugar
⅔ cup condensed milk
⅔ cup buttermilk
8 ounces white chocolate,
   chopped

1½ cups miniature
   marshmallows
2 cups Brazil nuts

Line 8x8-inch buttered baking pan with 2 sheets wax paper, extending ends over sides of pan. Butter wax paper. Combine sugar, condensed milk, and buttermilk in saucepan. Bring to a boil over medium heat, stirring constantly. Boil 7 minutes, stirring constantly. Remove from heat. Add chocolate and marshmallows, stirring till melted. Stir in nuts. Pour into prepared pan, spreading evenly. Let stand till cooled completely. Chill, covered, in refrigerator. Invert candy onto cutting surface; remove wax paper. Cut into squares. Yields 36 servings.

Sue B. Wofford, Columbus Council (Lawfully Good Eating)

Fabulous Fudge

2¼ cups sugar
¾ cup evaporated milk
16 large marshmallows
¼ cup margarine

¼ teaspoon salt
6 ounces chocolate chips
1 cup chopped nuts
1 teaspoon vanilla

Mix first 5 ingredients in large saucepan. Cook, stirring constantly, over medium heat to a boil. Boil and stir 5 minutes more. Remove from heat. Stir in chocolate chips till completely melted. Stir in nuts and vanilla. Spread in buttered 8-inch square pan. Cool; cut into squares.

Suzanne Howell, General (Dogwood Delights)

Mom's Fudge

PART 1:
3 (5-ounce) Hershey's bars, broken up
2 (12-ounce) packages milk chocolate chips

1 (7-ounce) jar marshmallow crème
2 cups chopped walnuts

PART 2:
1 (12-ounce) can evaporated milk

4 cups sugar
1½ sticks butter

Put Part 1 ingredients in large bowl and mix together. Bring Part 2 ingredients to a boil for 5 minutes, stirring constantly. Pour Part 2 over Part 1 and mix together till blended. Put in boxes lined with wax paper or glass dish lightly greased with butter. Makes approximately 6 pounds fudge.

Linda Clabaugh, Blue Ridge, GA (Great Southern Recipes)

Peanut Butter Fudge

3 cups sugar
¾ cup margarine
1 cup evaporated milk
1 cup chunky peanut butter
1 (7-ounce) jar marshmallow
   crème
1 teaspoon vanilla
½ cup chopped roasted peanuts

Combine sugar, margarine, and milk in saucepan; bring to a rolling boil, stirring constantly. Boil 5 minutes over medium heat, stirring constantly. Remove from heat and add peanut butter, mixing well. Add marshmallow crème, vanilla, and peanuts. Beat till well blended. Pour into greased 9x13-inch pan. Cool; cut in squares.

Barbara Keel, Conyers, GA (Great Southern Recipes)

White Trash

1 (12-ounce) package semisweet
   chocolate chips
1 cup peanut butter
1 stick margarine
1 (7-ounce) box Golden Graham
   cereal
1 (12-ounce) jar dry roasted
   peanuts
1 box golden raisins
1 teaspoon vanilla
1 (1-pound) box powdered sugar

Melt chocolate chips, peanut butter, and margarine on LOW in microwave. Drizzle over dry ingredients; add vanilla and mix well. Pour into white trash bag. Add powdered sugar and shake till well coated.

Betty Lovin, Decatur-Tucker (Dogwood Delights II)

Divinity

2 egg whites
2½ cups sugar
½ cup light corn syrup

½ cup water
¼ teaspoon salt
1 teaspoon vanilla

Beat egg whites till stiff. Combine sugar, corn syrup, water, and salt in heavy saucepan. Cook to soft-ball stage. Pour slowly over egg whites, beating constantly. Add vanilla. Continue beating until mixture holds shape. Drop from spoon onto wax paper. DO NOT MAKE ON A RAINY DAY.

Marilyn Long, Brookwood-Downtown (Dogwood Delights)

Pies and Other Desserts

1980
Cordless

Cordless phones first appeared around 1980 and were primitive by today's standards. These phones, without cables or cords, chiefly used radio frequency and were initially given a frequency of 27 MHz by the Federal Communications Commission (FCC), which is the same frequency range used by CB radio. The base needs a separate power source to transmit the signal to the handset. The cordless handset is powered by a battery that is recharged by the base station. By 1998 Caller ID was introduced, 2.4 GHz frequencies opened, and a Digital Spread Spectrum signal became available. This added security and spread the signal 360 degrees from the base to the handset, so there were no dead spots and distance could go to a quarter mile. As additional features were added, prices dropped and demand rose. Consumers now wanted all their phones to be cordless. This created a new set of problems. If there was ever a power failure, you wouldn't have any working phones.

Blueberry Pie

1 cup chopped pecans
2 pie shells, unbaked
1 (8-ounce) package cream
  cheese, softened
1 cup powdered sugar

1–2 teaspoons lemon juice
1 teaspoon milk
1 (21-ounce) can blueberry pie
  filling
1 (8-ounce) container Cool Whip

Spread pecans on bottom of pie shells and bake according to package directions; cool slightly. Mix together cream cheese, sugar, juice, and milk. Spread on pie shells. Spread blueberry pie filling on top of mixture as thick as you desire. Top with Cool Whip and refrigerate overnight. Serve cold.

Doris Weatherby, Chamblee-North Fulton (Dogwood Delights)

Strawberry Pie

1 (14-ounce) can condensed
  milk
⅓ cup lemon juice
1 (10-ounce) carton frozen
  strawberries, thawed

1 cup chopped pecans
1 (12-ounce) carton Cool Whip
2 graham cracker pie crusts

Mix condensed milk and lemon juice. Add strawberries, juice and all, and nuts; mix well. Fold in Cool Whip. Spoon into pie crust. Chill 3–4 hours. Can be frozen and taken out when needed.

Howard Robinson, Conyers, GA (Great Southern Recipes)

Pumpkin or Potato Pies

2 cups mashed cooked pumpkin
  or sweet potatoes
1½ cups sugar
3 tablespoons all-purpose flour
½ cup butter, melted
3 eggs, beaten

1 (5-ounce) can evaporated milk
1 teaspoon vanilla
2 unbaked 9-inch pie shells
Brown sugar and cinnamon for
  top

Combine pumpkin or potatoes, sugar, and flour in bowl; mix well.
Add butter, eggs, evaporated milk, and vanilla; mix well. Spoon
into pie shells. Sprinkle tops with brown sugar and cinnamon.
Bake at 350° for 30–40 minutes, or till brown. Yields 8 servings.

Maggie Cameron, Macon Council (Lawfully Good Eating)

Buttermilk Pie

½ cup Bisquick
½ cup sugar
3 eggs, beaten
⅓ cup butter, softened

1 cup buttermilk
1½ tablespoons vanilla
1 (9-inch) pie crust

Mix Bisquick and sugar; add eggs. Add butter and mix until well
blended. Add buttermilk and vanilla; mix well. Pour into pie
crust. Bake at 350° for 35–45 minutes.

June A. Robinson, Tucker, GA (Great Southern Recipes)

Sour Cream Pie

2 egg yolks
1 cup sugar
1 cup raisins
1 cup sour cream

1 teaspoon cinnamon
1 teaspoon ground cloves
1 unbaked 9-inch pie shell

Combine egg yolks and sugar in mixer bowl; mix well. Add raisins, sour cream, cinnamon, and cloves; mix well. Pour into unbaked pie shell. Bake at 400° for 20–25 minutes, or till brown. May top with meringue, if desired. Yields 8 servings.

Caroline Holley-Sampson, Athens-Gainesville Council
(Lawfully Good Eating)

Soda Cracker Dessert

1 stack saltine crackers,
  crushed
2 cups sugar
2 cups chopped pecans
6 egg whites, beaten
1 (15-ounce) can crushed
  pineapple, drained

1 (12-ounce) container whipped
  topping
1 (7-ounce) can flaked coconut
Maraschino cherries (optional)

Combine cracker crumbs, sugar, pecans, and egg whites; mix well. Spread in greased 9x12-inch baking dish. Bake at 400° till golden brown. Cool in pan. Layer pineapple, whipped topping, and coconut over crust. Top with cherries. Yields 15 servings.

Marsha Norton, Athens-Gainesville Council
(Lawfully Good Eating)

Million Dollar Pie

1 (8-ounce) carton Cool Whip
1 (15-ounce) can crushed
pineapple, drained
1 (14-ounce) can condensed
milk

1 cup chopped pecans
2 graham cracker crusts

Combine Cool Whip, pineapple, condensed milk, and pecans. Pour into pie shells and refrigerate till ready to serve.

Note: May substitute Mandarin oranges for pineapple.

Hazel Findley, General (Dogwood Delights); Faye Palmer,
Athens-Gainesville Council (Lawfully Good Eating)

Chocolate Chess Pie

1 cup sugar
3 tablespoons cornmeal
3 tablespoon cocoa
3 whole eggs, well beaten

½ cup butter, melted
½ cup white corn syrup
1 teaspoon vanilla
1 (9-inch) pie shell

Mix first 3 ingredients in bowl. Add next 4 ingredients. Mix well and pour into pie shell. Bake in 325°–350° oven 45 minutes. Chill before slicing. Serves 8.

Mallory Magwood, General (Dogwood Delights)

Chess Pie

3 eggs
1½ cups sugar
1 stick butter, melted
3 tablespoons cornmeal

5 tablespoons milk
2 tablespoons lemon juice
1 (9-inch) pie shell

Beat eggs; add sugar and butter; mix well. Add remaining ingredients. Pour into pie shell and bake at 300° for 45–50 minutes.

Reba Bradley, General (Dogwood Delights)

Key Lime Pie

1 (14-ounce) can condensed
  milk
4 eggs, separated
½ cup lime juice

6 tablespoons sugar
½ teaspoon cream of tartar
1 (9-inch) pie shell, baked

Combine milk, egg yolks, and lime juice. Beat 1 egg white stiff and fold into creamy mixture.

Beat remaining 3 egg whites and gradually add sugar and cream of tartar. Place filling into baked pie shell and add meringue. Bake at 350° till meringue is golden brown.

Mrs. John. B. White, General (Dogwood Delights); Chuck Baker,
Gainesville Life Member Club (Lawfully Good Eating)

Mandarin Orange Pie

2 (11-ounce) cans Mandarin
  oranges, drained
1 (8-ounce) can crushed
  pineapple, drained
1 cup chopped nuts
½ cup ReaLemon

1 (14-ounce) can condensed
  milk
1 (12-ounce) container Cool
  Whip
2 (8-inch) graham cracker
  crusts

Mix oranges, pineapple, nuts, lemon juice, and condensed milk. Fold in Cool Whip; mix well. Pour into graham cracker pie shells. Refrigerate 1 hour.

Barbara Camp, Austell-Marietta (Dogwood Delights II)

Lemon Meringue Pie

1 cup sugar
¼ cup cornstarch
¼ teaspoon salt
1½ cups boiling water
2 egg yolks
⅓ cup lemon juice

1 tablespoon grated lemon rind
1 tablespoon butter
1 (9-inch) pie shell, baked
3 egg whites
5 tablespoons sugar (for
  meringue)

Combine sugar, cornstarch, and salt in top of double boiler. Add water gradually and cook over boiling water until thick, stirring constantly. Cover and cook 15 minutes more. Gradually pour half the mixture over beaten egg yolks. Cook 5 minutes. Add lemon juice, rind, and butter; stir well and pour into pie shell. Beat egg whites; gradually add sugar. Beat until stiff. Cover pie with meringue. Bake at 350° till meringue is golden brown.

Margaret Knight, General (Dogwood Delights)

Egg Custard Pie

1 tablespoon flour
Pinch of salt
1½ cups sugar
⅓ cup margarine, melted

¼ cup buttermilk
1 teaspoon vanilla
3 eggs, slightly beaten

Mix flour, salt, and sugar. Add margarine, buttermilk, vanilla, and eggs. Pour into pie pan. Bake at 350° about 40 minutes. Buttermilk will make a thin crust when cooled.

Lorine Vernon, General (Dogwood Delights)

Coconut Cream Pie

⅔ cup sugar
½ teaspoon salt
2½ tablespoons cornstarch
1 tablespoon flour
3 cups milk
3 egg yolks, beaten
1 cup shredded moist flaked
coconut, divided

1½ teaspoons vanilla
1 tablespoon butter
1 (9-inch) pie crust
Meringue (made with remaining
egg whites)

Mix sugar, salt, cornstarch, and flour in saucepan. Add milk and cook over moderate heat, stirring constantly till mixture thickens and boils. Boil 1 minute. Remove from heat. Stir at least 1 cup hot mixture slowly into egg yolks. Add to mixture and boil 1 more minute, stirring constantly. Remove from heat and stir in ¾ cup coconut, vanilla, and butter. Pour into pie crust. Top with meringue; run under broiler to brown peaks. Sprinkle with remaining coconut. Chill.

Cathy Ecker, Chamblee-North Fulton (Dogwood Delights)

Never Fail Crustless Coconut Pie

4 eggs
1¼ cups sugar
½ cup self-rising flour
¼ stick butter, melted

1 cup flaked coconut
1 (12-ounce) can evaporated
  milk
1 teaspoon vanilla

Beat eggs; blend in sugar and flour. Add remaining ingredients. Pour into 9-inch greased pie pan. Bake at 350° for 30–40 minutes till knife comes out clean.

Note: This pie makes its own crust. Also, makes egg custard by omitting coconut.

Shirley Cody, Chamblee-North Fulton (Dogwood Delights II)

Chocolate Pie

4 tablespoons cocoa
3 eggs, separated
1 cup sugar

2 teaspoons flour
1½ cups milk
1 (8-inch) pie shell, baked

Cook and stir cocoa, beaten egg yolks, sugar, flour, and milk till thick. Pour into pie shell. Make meringue with remaining egg whites. Top with meringue and bake in 350° oven till brown.

Willene Berry, Austell-Marietta (Dogwood Delights II)

German Chocolate Pies

4 ounces German sweet
  chocolate
½ cup butter
1 (12-ounce) can evaporated
  milk
1½ cups sugar

2 eggs, beaten
3 tablespoons cornstarch
1 teaspoon vanilla
1½ cups flaked coconut
½ cup chopped pecans
2 unbaked 9-inch pie shells

Melt chocolate and butter together in saucepan over low heat. Remove from heat. Gradually add evaporated milk, beating well. Add sugar, eggs, cornstarch, and vanilla; beat well. Sprinkle coconut and pecans into pie shells. Top with chocolate mixture. Bake at 375° for 30 minutes. May also mix coconut and pecans into chocolate mixture. Yields 8 servings.

Betty Conley, Athens-Gainesville Council
(Lawfully Good Eating)

In 1978, American Telephone and Telegraph's (AT&T) Bell Laboratories began testing a mobile telephone system based on hexagonal geographical regions called cells. As the caller's vehicle passed from one cell to another, an automatic switching system would transfer the telephone call to another cell without interruption. The cellular telephone system began nationwide usage in the United States in 1983.

Triple Chocolate S'More Pie

1¼ cups graham cracker
  crumbs
¼ cup sugar
⅓ cup butter, melted
1 cup milk chocolate chips
1½ cups condensed milk,
  divided

1½ teaspoons vanilla extract,
  divided
1 cup white chocolate chips
1 cup dark chocolate chips
1½ cups miniature
  marshmallows

Preheat oven to 375°. Spray 9-inch pie pan with nonstick cooking spray. In a bowl, combine graham cracker crumbs, sugar, and butter. Press mixture firmly into sprayed pie pan, covering bottom and sides. Bake 6–8 minutes; set aside to cool.

In a microwave-safe bowl, combine milk chocolate chips, ½ cup condensed milk, and ½ teaspoon vanilla. Microwave 2 minutes. Stir till all chips are melted; pour into cooled crust. Set in fridge while preparing second layer.

Repeat above process using white chocolate chips (microwave only 1½ minutes). Pour over milk chocolate layer. Set in fridge while preparing third layer.

Repeat above process using dark chocolate chips. Pour over white chocolate layer.

Preheat broiler. Evenly cover top layer with miniature marshmallows. Place under broiler for a few minutes, just till marshmallows are lightly browned. Refrigerate at least 1 hour. Yields 16 slices.

Brenda Borland, Social Circle, GA (Great Southern Recipes)

Fudge Brownie Pie

1 (9-inch) unbaked pastry shell
1 cup semisweet chocolate
  chips
¼ cup butter
1 (14-ounce) can condensed
  milk
½ cup biscuit baking mix
2 eggs
1 teaspoon vanilla
1 cup chopped nuts

Preheat oven to 375°. Bake pastry shell 10 minutes; remove from oven. Reduce heat to 325°. In saucepan over low heat, melt chips with butter. In large mixer bowl, beat chocolate mixture with remaining ingredients, except nuts, till smooth. Add nuts. Pour into prepared pastry shell. Bake 35–40 minutes, or till center is set. Cool slightly. Serve with ice cream, if desired. Refrigerate leftovers.

Wilma Smith Davis, General (Dogwood Delights II)

Apple Pie

⅔ cup sugar (1 cup if apples
  are tart)
2 tablespoons all-purpose flour
¼ teaspoon salt
1½ teaspoons cinnamon
4–6 large apples, peeled, sliced
2 (9-inch) pie crusts, unbaked
1 tablespoon butter

Mix sugar, flour, salt, and cinnamon in large bowl. Combine dry ingredients with sliced apples; stir and let sit 15–20 minutes to make juicy.

Fill bottom of unbaked pie crust with mixture. Dot with butter. Cover with top pie crust. Bake in preheated 450° oven 15 minutes. Reduce heat to 350° and bake 45 minutes longer.

Jane Bridges, Area (Dogwood Delights II)

Banana Split Pie

3 sticks margarine, divided
2 cups graham cracker crumbs
7 large bananas
1 (20-ounce) can crushed
  pineapple, drained
2 eggs

2 cups powdered sugar
1 teaspoon vanilla
2 cups Cool Whip
1 (4½-ounce) jar maraschino
  cherries, drained
1 cup chopped nuts

Melt 1 stick margarine. Pour over graham cracker crumbs. Stir and press into 9x13-inch pan to make crust. Cut bananas and place over crust. Spread pineapple over bananas. Beat eggs, powdered sugar, remaining 2 sticks softened margarine, and vanilla till well mixed. Spread over mixture. Put Cool Whip on top. Place cherries and nuts on top. Sprinkle with additional cracker crumbs, if desired.

Barbara Cosby, Austell-Marietta (Dogwood Delights II)

Crunchy Apple Crisp

8 apples, peeled, sliced
1 stick butter
½ cup brown sugar
½ teaspoon cinnamon
2 cups all-purpose flour
2 cups sugar

1 teaspoon salt
2 teaspoons baking powder
1 cup oil
2 eggs, beaten
Coconut (optional)

Spread sliced apples on bottom of aluminum foil-lined or buttered 9x13-inch pan, and dot with butter; sprinkle with brown sugar and cinnamon. Sift together flour, sugar, salt, and baking powder. Mix oil and eggs and add to flour mixture, mixing lightly. Spread over apples. Top with coconut, if desired. Bake 40 minutes at 350° or till top is crunchy.

Mary Townsend, Chamblee-North Fulton (Dogwood Delights)

Cheesy Apples

1 (16-ounce) can sliced apples
½ cup butter, melted
½–1 cup sugar
¾ cup all-purpose flour

8 ounces Velveeta cheese,
  shredded
¼ cup milk

Arrange apples in casserole dish. Mix melted butter, sugar, flour, cheese, and milk. Spread over apples. Bake at 350° for 30–40 minutes or till apples are tender. Yields 6 servings.

Linda Ramey, Athens-Gainesville Council
(Lawfully Good Eating)

Easy Peach Cobbler

2 cups sugar, divided
2 cups sliced fresh peaches
1 stick butter

¾ cup all-purpose flour
2 teaspoons baking powder
¾ cup milk

Mix 1 cup sugar with peaches; let soak. Melt butter in deep casserole dish. Mix flour, baking powder, remaining 1 cup sugar, and milk together well. Pour mixture over butter. Do not stir. Add peaches. Still do not stir. Bake 1 hour at 350°.

Charlene Lankford, General (Dogwood Delights)

Fast Blueberry Cobbler

1 stick margarine
1 cup self-rising flour
1 cup sugar, divided

¾ cup milk
2 cups fresh blueberries
½ cup water

Heat oven to 350°. In 1½-quart baking dish, melt butter. In mixing bowl, combine flour, ½ cup sugar, and milk; pour evenly over butter. Combine berries, remaining ½ cup sugar, and water; spoon evenly over flour mixture. Do not stir. Bake 40–45 minutes.

Faye Stephens, Decatur-Tucker (Dogwood Delights II)

Georgia Peach Cobbler

1 quart sliced peaches
2 cups sugar, divided
1 cup self-rising flour

3 tablespoons oil
½ cup milk
1 cup hot water

Arrange peaches in baking dish. Sprinkle with ½ cup sugar. Mix flour, ½ cup sugar, oil, and milk in bowl. Pour over peaches. Sprinkle with remaining 1 cup sugar. Pour hot water over all. Bake at 375° for 1 hour or till light brown. Yields 8 servings.

Virginia Stembridge, Macon Council (Lawfully Good Eating)

Hot Fruit Casserole

1 (15-ounce) can pear halves
1 (15-ounce) can peach halves
1 (15-ounce) can apricots
1 (15-ounce) can pineapple
  chunks
1 (10-ounce) jar maraschino
  cherries
1 stick butter
¾ cup brown sugar

Drain all fruit overnight. Place fruit in casserole dish. Melt butter and brown sugar together and pour over fruit. Bake at 350° for 45 minutes.

Jerry Farkas, Marietta, GA (Great Southern Recipes)

Strawberry Crunch

CRUST:
2 cups graham cracker crumbs   1½ sticks butter, melted

Mix graham cracker crumbs and butter. Press into 8x8-inch dish. Set in oven for 3–4 minutes at 350°. Let cool.

FILLING:
1 (8-ounce) package cream
  cheese, softened
1 cup powdered sugar
¼ cup milk
2 cups chopped nuts
1 (10-ounce) package frozen
  strawberries

Beat cream cheese, sugar, and milk till smooth. Add nuts and pour over Crust. Pour frozen strawberries on top.

TOPPING:
2 packages Dream Whip   1 cup milk

Beat ingredients till peaks form. Put Topping on Filling.

Sheila Hull, Area (Dogwood Delights II)

Strawberry Mile-High Dessert

1 cup all-purpose flour	½ cup sugar
¼ cup packed brown sugar	2 egg whites
½ cup chopped pecans	1 tablespoon lemon juice
½ cup margarine, melted	⅛ teaspoon salt
1 (10-ounce) package frozen	½ cup whipping cream
strawberries, partially	1 teaspoon vanilla extract
thawed	

Mix flour, brown sugar, pecans, and margarine in bowl till crumbly. Place in 9x9-inch baking pan. Bake at 350° for 10 minutes, stirring frequently. Cool to room temperature. Reserve ⅓ of the crumb mixture. Pat remaining crumbs into smooth layer. Combine strawberries, sugar, egg whites, lemon juice, and salt in large mixer bowl. Beat 15 minutes, beginning at low speed and increasing speed gradually till mixture forms stiff peaks. Whip cream with vanilla in bowl. Fold into strawberry mixture. Spoon into prepared pan. Sprinkle with reserved crumbs. Freeze till serving time. Yields 9 servings.

Jonnie Josie, Columbus Council (Lawfully Good Eating)

Strawberry-Raspberry Dessert

1 cup margarine, softened
2 cups sugar, divided
2 cups crushed pretzels
1 (16-ounce) carton Cool whip
2 (8-ounce) packages cream
  cheese, softened

1 (6-ounce) package strawberry
  or raspberry Jell-O
2 cups boiling water
1 (10-ounce) package frozen
  strawberries or raspberries
1 (8-ounce) carton Cool Whip

Cream together margarine and 1 cup sugar. Add crushed pretzels. Spread in a 9x13-inch pan. Bake at 325° for 10 minutes.

Cream together remaining 1 cup sugar, 16 ounces Cool Whip, and cream cheese. Spread over cooled pretzel layer.

Dissolve Jell-O with 2 cups boiling water. Add frozen berries to Jell-O. Let stand till slightly thickened. Put a layer of this mixture on top of cream cheese layer. Chill. When ready to serve, cover the Jell-O layer with remaining carton of Cool Whip.

Tom Wolfe, Alpharetta, GA (Great Southern Recipes)

Pecan Pie

½ cup sugar
1 cup dark Karo syrup
3 whole eggs
1 cup pecans

4 teaspoons butter
1 teaspoon vanilla
¼ teaspoon salt
1 (9-inch) unbaked pie shell

Combine sugar and syrup in saucepan. Cook to 228°, stirring constantly. Beat eggs; add syrup mixture. Add remaining ingredients. Pour into pie shell. Bake at 450° for 10 minutes, then at 300° for 35 minutes. (Use aluminum foil around edge of pie crust to prevent burning.)

Janet Pratt, General (Dogwood Delights)

Nutty Chocolate Delight

FIRST LAYER:

1 cup self-rising flour   ½ cup chopped nuts
1 stick margarine, softened

Combine till crumbly and pat in bottom of 8x12-inch pan. Bake at 325° for 15 minutes. Cool.

SECOND LAYER:

1 cup powdered sugar   ½ (12-ounce) container Cool
1 (8-ounce) package cream   Whip
   cheese, softened

Mix well and spread over First Layer.

THIRD LAYER:

2 (3-ounce) packages chocolate   3 cups milk
   instant pudding

Combine ingredients and pour over Second Layer.

FOURTH LAYER:

½ (12-ounce) container Cool   1 cup chopped nuts
   Whip

Top with Cool Whip, and sprinkle with chopped nuts. Serve in squares.

Sara Herndon, Decatur-Tucker (Dogwood Delights II)

River Room Lemon Tart

This is a very easy and elegant dessert.

2 cups graham cracker crumbs
⅔ cup sugar
½ stick butter, melted
4 (14-ounce) cans condensed
  milk

8 egg yolks
1 cup freshly squeezed lemon
  juice

Preheat oven to 350°. Combine graham cracker crumbs, sugar, and butter. Press into well-greased 10-inch springform pan, evenly covering bottom of pan. Bake 10–15 minutes. Remove from oven and cool completely. Preheat oven to 250° for convection and 275° for standard.

With electric mixer, combine condensed milk, egg yolks, and lemon juice; mix thoroughly. Pour filling over cooled crust and bake 30 minutes. Remove from oven and cool. Refrigerate 2–3 hours before serving.

Optional: Purée frozen raspberries and pour a little over each serving.

Doris Thompson, Grayson, GA (Great Southern Recipes)

Rice Pudding

1¼ cups water
½ cup rice
½ teaspoon salt
2 cups milk
2 eggs, beaten

⅓ cup sugar
1 teaspoon vanilla
¼ cup raisins, steamed,
    drained

Bring water to a boil; stir in rice and salt. Cover and simmer till water is absorbed, about 30 minutes. Add milk and boil gently, stirring occasionally, till thickened slightly, about 5 minutes. Combine eggs, sugar, and vanilla. Gradually stir in rice mixture. Mix well. Stir in raisins. Pour into greased 1½-quart casserole. Place in pan of hot water. Bake uncovered 45–50 minutes at 350°, or till knife comes out clean.

Sandra Bramblett, Long Lines-AT&T Communications
(Dogwood Delights)

Banana Pudding

¾ cup sugar, divided
3 tablespoons all-purpose flour
Dash of salt
4 eggs (3 separated)

2 cups milk
½ teaspoon vanilla extract
Vanilla wafers
5–6 bananas

Combine ½ cup sugar, flour, and salt in saucepan. Mix in 1 whole egg and 3 egg whites. Slowly stir in milk. Cook, stirring constantly, till thickened. Remove from heat; add vanilla. Place wafers and bananas in layers in a 1½-quart casserole dish. Pour cooked mixture over bananas and wafers. Beat remaining 3 egg whites till stiff. Gradually add remaining ¼ cup sugar; beat till mixture forms stiff peaks. Pile on top of pudding. Bake in preheated 425° oven 5 minutes, or till browned on top.

Kathy Edwards, Chamblee-North Fulton (Dogwood Delights II)

Strawberry Pudding

1½ pints strawberries
¾ cup sugar
3 tablespoons all-purpose flour

2 cups milk
2 eggs, separated
40 or more vanilla wafers

Wash, stem, and halve strawberries. Mix sugar and flour in saucepan. Add part of the milk and blend till smooth. Add beaten egg yolks and rest of milk. Cook over low heat, stirring constantly, till custard starts to thicken.

Line bottom and sides of baking dish with vanilla wafers. Add a layer of half the strawberries, then half the boiled custard. Repeat layer of wafers, rest of strawberries, and rest of custard. Beat egg whites till stiff. Add 4 tablespoons sugar and beat well. Spread on top of pudding. Bake in preheated 375° oven till meringue is golden brown. Makes 6–8 servings.

Pat Gulley, Decatur-Tucker (Dogwood Delights II)

Orange Fluff

1 (11-ounce) can Mandarin
oranges, well drained
1 (20-ounce) can crushed
pineapple, well drained
1 (3-ounce) box orange Jell-O

1 (8-ounce) container cottage
cheese
1 cup chopped pecans
1 (12-ounce) carton Cool Whip

Cut up Mandarin oranges and combine with pineapple in mixing bowl. Add Jell-O and fold in cottage cheese. Add pecans and Cool Whip; mix well. Put in covered container and refrigerate several hours.

Mary Wright, Hapeville, GA (Great Southern Recipes)

Peach Ice Cream

4 cups peeled, diced fresh
  peaches (about 8 small
  ripe peaches)
1 cup sugar
1 (12-ounce) can evaporated
  milk

1 (4-ounce) package vanilla
  instant pudding mix
1 (14-ounce) can condensed
  milk
4 cups half-and-half

Combine peaches and sugar; let stand 1 hour. Process peach mixture in food processor till smooth, stopping to scrape down sides. Stir together evaporated milk and pudding mix in large bowl. Stir in peach purée, condensed milk, and half-and-half.

Pour mixture into freezer container for a 4-quart freezer; freeze according to manufacturer's instructions. Spoon into airtight container and freeze till firm. Makes 2 quarts.

Doris Thompson, Grayson, GA (Great Southern Recipes)

Butter Pecan Ice Cream

3 cups sugar
2 tablespoons (heaping)
  all-purpose flour
2 (12-ounce) cans evaporated
  milk
2 (14-ounce) cans condensed
  milk

5 eggs
1½ teaspoons butternut
  flavoring
1½–2 cups buttered toasted
  pecans

Mix sugar and flour in bowl. Add evaporated milk, condensed milk, eggs, and flavoring; mix well. Stir in pecans. Pour into ice cream freezer container. Freeze using manufacturer's directions. Yields 10 servings.

Jan Snider, Buena Vista Council (Lawfully Good Eating)

Chocolate Pizza

2 cups semisweet chocolate
  chips
16 ounces white almond bark,
  divided
1 cup crisp rice cereal

1 cup chopped pecans
2 cups miniature marshmallows
Red and green cherries
⅓ cup flaked coconut
1 teaspoon oil

Melt chocolate with 14 ounces almond bark in saucepan over low heat; remove from heat. Stir in cereal and pecans. Add marshmallows; mix well. Pour into greased 12-inch pizza pan. Top with cherries. Sprinkle with coconut. Melt remaining 2 ounces almond bark with oil in saucepan over low heat, stirring till smooth. Drizzle over coconut. Chill till firm. Cut into wedges. Yields 16 servings.

Lana Wilson, Valdosta Council (Lawfully Good Eating)

Sweetened Condensed Milk

1 cup instant nonfat milk
  powder
½ cup boiling water

⅔ cup sugar
3 tablespoons margarine

Place all ingredients in blender container. Process at high speed till smooth. Use in any recipe calling for commercially sold sweetened condensed milk. Makes 1¼ cups (10 ounces) and contains 1,205 calories.

Carol Ennis, Area (Dogwood Delights II)

Equivalents, Substitutions, Etc.

EQUIVALENTS:

Apple: 1 medium = 1 cup chopped

Banana: 1 medium = $\frac{1}{3}$ cup

Berries: 1 pint = $1\frac{3}{4}$ cups

Bread: 1 slice = $\frac{1}{2}$ cup soft crumbs = $\frac{1}{4}$ cup fine, dry crumbs

Broth, beef or chicken: 1 cup = 1 bouillon cube dissolved in 1 cup boiling water

Butter: 1 stick = $\frac{1}{4}$ pound = $\frac{1}{2}$ cup

Cabbage: 2 pounds = 9 cups shredded or 5 cups cooked

Cheese, grated: 1 pound = 4 cups; 8 ounces = 2 cups

Chicken: 1 large boned breast = 2 cups cooked meat

Chocolate, bitter: 1 square or 1 ounce = 2 tablespoons grated

Coconut: $3\frac{1}{2}$-ounce can = $1\frac{1}{3}$ cups

Cool Whip: 8 ounces = 3 cups

Cornmeal: 1 pound = 3 cups

Crabmeat, fresh: 1 pound = 3 cups

Crackers, graham: 15 = 1 cup crushed

Crackers, saltine: 23 = 1 cup crushed

Cream, heavy: 1 cup = 2–$2\frac{1}{2}$ cups whipped

Cream cheese: 3 ounces = $6\frac{2}{3}$ tablespoons

Egg whites: 8–10 = 1 cup

Eggs: 4–5 = 1 cup

Evaporated milk: $5\frac{1}{3}$-ounce can = $\frac{2}{3}$ cup; 12-ounce can = $1\frac{1}{4}$ cups

Flour: 1 pound = $4\frac{1}{2}$ cups

Flour, self-rising: 1 cup = 1 cup all-purpose + $1\frac{1}{2}$ teaspoons baking powder + $\frac{1}{2}$ teaspoon salt

Garlic powder: $\frac{1}{8}$ teaspoon = 1 average clove

Gingerroot: 1 teaspoon = $\frac{3}{4}$ teaspoon ground

Grits: 1 cup = 4 cups cooked

Herbs, fresh: 1 tablespoon = 1 teaspoon dried

Lemon: 1 medium = 3 tablespoons juice

Marshmallows: $\frac{1}{4}$ pound = 16 large; $\frac{1}{2}$ cup = 4 large

Milk, whole: 1 cup = $\frac{1}{2}$ cup evaporated + $\frac{1}{2}$ cup water

Mushrooms: $\frac{1}{4}$ pound fresh = 1 cup sliced

Mustard, dry: 1 teaspoon = 1 tablespoon prepared

Noodles: 1 pound = 7 cups cooked

Nuts, chopped: $\frac{1}{4}$ pound = 1 cup

Onion: 1 medium = $\frac{3}{4}$–1 cup chopped = 2 tablespoons dried chopped (flakes)

Orange: 3–4 medium = 1 cup juice

Pecans: 1 pound shelled = 4 cups

Potatoes: 1 pound = 3 medium

Rice: 1 cup = 3 cups cooked

Spaghetti: 1 pound uncooked = 5 cups cooked

Spinach, fresh: 2 cups chopped = 1 (10-ounce) package frozen chopped

Sugar, brown: 1 pound = $2\frac{1}{2}$ cups

Sugar, powdered: 1 pound = $3\frac{1}{2}$ cups

Sugar, white: 1 pound = $2\frac{1}{4}$ cups

Vanilla wafers: 22 = 1 cup fine crumbs

Equivalents, Substitutions, Etc.

SUBSTITUTIONS:

1 slice cooked bacon = 1 tablespoon bacon bits

1 cup buttermilk = 1 cup plain yogurt; or 1 tablespoon lemon juice or vinegar + plain milk to make 1 cup

1 cup sifted cake flour = ⅞ cup sifted all-purpose flour

1 ounce unsweetened chocolate = 3 tablespoons cocoa + 1 tablespoon butter or margarine

1 ounce semisweet chocolate = 3 tablespoons cocoa + 1 tablespoon butter or margarine + 3 tablespoons sugar

1 tablespoon cornstarch = 2 tablespoons flour (for thickening)

1 cup heavy cream (for cooking, not whipping) = ⅓ cup butter + ¾ cup milk

1 cup sour cream = ⅓ cup milk + ⅓ cup butter; or 1 cup plain yogurt

1 cup tartar sauce = 6 tablespoons mayonnaise or salad dressing + 2 tablespoons pickle relish

1 cup tomato juice = ½ cup tomato sauce + ½ cup water

1 cup vegetable oil = ½ pound (2 sticks) butter

1 cup whipping cream, whipped = 6–8 ounces Cool Whip

1 cup whole milk = ½ cup evaporated milk + ½ cup water

MEASUREMENTS:

3 teaspoons = 1 tablespoon

1 tablespoon = ½ fluid ounce

2 tablespoons = ⅛ cup

3 tablespoons = 1 jigger

4 tablespoons = ¼ cup

8 tablespoons = ½ cup or 4 ounces

12 tablespoons = ¾ cup

16 tablespoons = 1 cup or 8 ounces

⅜ cup = ¼ cup + 2 tablespoons

⅝ cup = ½ cup + 2 tablespoons

⅞ cup = ¾ cup + 2 tablespoons

½ cup = 4 fluid ounces

1 cup = ½ pint or 8 fluid ounces

2 cups = 1 pint or 16 fluid ounces

1 pint, liquid = 2 cups or 16 fluid ounces

1 quart, liquid = 2 pints or 4 cups

1 gallon, liquid = 4 quarts or 8 pints or 16 cups

OVEN-TO-CROCKPOT CONVERSIONS:

15–30 minutes in the oven = 1½–2½ hours on HIGH or 4–6 hours on LOW

35–45 minutes in the oven = 2–3 hours on HIGH or 6–8 hours on LOW

50 minutes–3 hours in the oven = 4–5 hours on HIGH or 8–10 hours on LOW

Index

1983
Cellular

The development of commercial cellular systems did not occur rapidly—almost 36 years passed between the initial concept in 1947, and the first commercial systems in 1983. Delays due to regulatory discussions allowed developers to incorporate supporting technologies like microprocessors and integrated circuits into the cellular telephone as we know it. "Cellular" began as a term for analog service transferred from cell to cell, but now refers to all wireless phone services. Statistically, there were one million subscribers by 1987, increasing 1,000% by 1991 with both analog and digital capability. In 2008, there were more than 270 million wireless customers, who used more than 7.7 billion minutes per day.

Text messaging services appeared in 1993. Although "texting" started out slowly, it is now the most widely used and reliable mobile data service, with more than 3.5 billion text messages being sent out daily.

Index

Index

Index

Index

Index

Index

Index

BEST OF THE BEST STATE COOKBOOK SERIES

ALABAMA

ALASKA

ARIZONA

ARKANSAS

BIG SKY
Includes Montana, Wyoming

CALIFORNIA

COLORADO

FLORIDA

GEORGIA

GREAT PLAINS
Includes North Dakota,
South Dakota, Nebraska,
and Kansas

HAWAII

IDAHO

ILLINOIS

INDIANA

IOWA

KENTUCKY

LOUISIANA

LOUISIANA II

MICHIGAN

MID-ATLANTIC
Includes Maryland,
Delaware, New Jersey, and
Washington, D.C.

MINNESOTA

MISSISSIPPI

MISSOURI

NEVADA

NEW ENGLAND
Includes Rhode Island,
Connecticut, Massachusetts,
Vermont, New Hampshire,
and Maine

NEW MEXICO

NEW YORK

NO. CAROLINA

OHIO

OKLAHOMA

OREGON

PENNSYLVANIA

SO. CAROLINA

TENNESSEE

TEXAS

TEXAS II

UTAH

VIRGINIA

VIRGINIA II

WASHINGTON

WEST VIRGINIA

WISCONSIN

All Best of the Best Cookbooks are 6x9 inches, are comb-bound, contain over 400 recipes, and total 264–352 pages. Each contains illustrations, photographs, an index and a list of contributing cookbooks, a special feature which cookbook collectors enjoy. Scattered throughout the cookbooks are short quips that provide interesting information about each state, including historical facts and major attractions along with amusing trivia. Retail price per copy $16.95.

To order by credit card, call toll-free **1-800-343-1583**, visit **www.quailridge.com**, or use the Order Form below.

- -

Order Form

Send check, money order, or credit card info to:
QUAIL RIDGE PRESS • P. O. Box 123 • Brandon, MS 39043

Name _____

Address _____

City_____

State/Zip _____

Phone # _____

Email Address _____

❑ Check enclosed

Charge to: ❑ Visa ❑ MC ❑ AmEx ❑ Disc

Card # _____

Expiration Date _____

Signature _____

Qty.	Title of Book (State) or HOF set	Total

Subtotal _____

Mississippi residents add 7% sales tax _____

Postage ($4.00 any number of books) **+ $4.00**

TOTAL _____